PELICAN BOOKS

THE IDEA OF PROGRESS

Sidney Pollard is Professor of Economic History
in the University of Sh... ...s interests lie
in modern economic ... ...
Vice-President of th... ...
Studies, a past Chai... ...
Study of Labour Hi... ...
Bulletin.

The present work i... ...
at Sheffield University. Previous writ...
A History of Labour in Sheffield, *The Development
of the British Economy*, *1914–67*, *The Genesis of
Modern Management* (available as a Pelican), *The
Gold Standard and Employment Between the Wars*,
and *The Wealth of Britain 1085–1966* (with D. W.
Crossley).

Sidney Pollard

THE IDEA OF PROGRESS
History and Society

Penguin Books

Penguin Books Ltd, Harmondsworth, Middlesex, England
Penguin Books Inc., 7110 Ambassador Road, Baltimore, Maryland 21207, U.S.A.
Penguin Books Australia Ltd, Ringwood, Victoria, Australia

—

First published by C. A. Watts 1968
Published in Pelican Books 1971
Copyright © S. Pollard, 1968

—

Made and printed in Great Britain
by Hazell Watson & Viney Ltd
Aylesbury, Bucks
Set in Linotype Plantin

CONTENTS

... in the midst of their ravages manners are gradually softened, the human mind takes enlightenment, separate nations draw nearer to each other, commerce and policy connect at last all the parts of the globe, and the total mass of the human race ... marches always, although slowly, towards still higher perfection. (TURGOT, *On the Successive Advances of the Human Mind*, 1750)

Nature has set no term to the perfection of human faculties ... the perfectibility of man is truly infinite; and ... the progress of this perfectibility, from now on independent of any power that might wish to halt it, has no other limit than the duration of the globe upon which nature has cast us. (CONDORCET, *The Progress of the Human Mind*, 1794)

The imagination of the poets placed the Golden Age in the cradle of Mankind, in the ignorance and brutality of earlier times. It is rather the Iron Age which should be regulated there. The Golden Age of the human species is not behind us, it is before us. It lies in the perfection of the social order. Our fathers did not see it at all. Our children will one day arrive there. It is for us to clear the path. (SAINT-SIMON, *The Reorganisation of European Society*, 1814)

This constancy of progress, of progress in the direction of organized and assured freedom, is the characteristic fact of modern history, and its tribute to the theory of Providence. (Lord ACTON, *A Lecture on the Study of History*, 1895)

Le XVIIIᵉ siècle n'a pa seulement critiqué ... il a laissé au monde une trace de son action féconde; c'est l'idée de Progrès qui s'est realisé dans la Révolution et dans le régime moderne. (JULES DELVAILLE, *Essai sur l'histoire de l'idée de progrès*, 1910)

(There is) one certain judgement of value that can be made about history, and that is *the idea of progress*. If this great human truth were once more to be frankly accepted, the reason for it, and the consequences of it, consistently and imaginatively explored and taught, history would not only be an infinitely richer education but also play a much more effective part in the culture of western society. (J. H. PLUMB, 'The Historian's Dilemma', 1964)

PREFACE

THE world today believes in progress. Indeed, so widespread is this belief among modern nations, that Governments will ignore it at their peril, and the word 'progress' itself has become an unqualified term of praise. As is usual in such cases of general approval an even superficial inquiry will quickly reveal that the term of 'progress' may take in a host of different meanings. It will also reveal that the belief in it is very recent, having become significant only in the past three hundred years or so, and that those who might be expected to have devoted most time to its consideration, the historians and philosophers of history, are the least certain of its validity.

A belief in progress implies that things will in some sense get better in the future, but it has never been limited to this simple idea of melioration. It is, to begin with, never a belief in a religious sense, as a dogma, nor is it based on the hope of a conjunction of favourable accidents. It is, instead, always in the nature of a scientific prediction, based on the reading of history, or at least recent history, and the operation of laws of social development. Thus a belief in progress implies the assumption that a pattern of change exists in the history of mankind, that this pattern is known, that it consists of irreversible changes in one general direction only, and that this direction is towards improvement from 'a less to a more desirable state of affairs'.[1]

'The idea of human progress then is a theory which involves a synthesis of the past and a prophecy of the future.'[2] But its corollaries are more far-reaching than this. It implies a belief in

1. These are all the definitions underlying the work of CHARLES VAN DOREN, *The Idea of Progress* (New York, 1967), especially pp. 4–6.
2. J. B. BURY, *The Idea of Progress* (1920), p. 5.

9

a rational understanding, a 'science' of history, a possibility of deducing generalizations which will remain valid for at least a considerable time into the future, and therefore a degree, at least, of determinism, and both these doctrines have been bitterly opposed by many historians and philosophers in the past. It implies, further, the belief that historical generalizations are valid for all humanity, so that even if it can be shown that the history of the nations is a history of variety rather than unity, this is only so because they are at different points along the same, or closely parallel, routes and not, as has from time to time been suggested, different civilizations obeying quite distinct sets of laws. Historians holding to the concept of progress, therefore, will tend to stress long-term, fundamental socio-economic changes, rather than the temporary fluctuation in political power. Finally, the belief in progress also implies a scale of values outside the areas of history itself, and not historically conditioned, against which the improvement postulated by 'progress' may be measured.

Before the seventeenth century few of these propositions would have commanded very widespread, or indeed any, assent. Even in the course of the past three centuries, there have been philosophers and churchmen, politicians and historians who have bitterly denounced them, while yet with less than perfect consistency, proclaiming their support for 'progress'. Nor is the widespread support today necessarily based on rational philosophical convictions. Instead, it often goes little farther than an assurance that science and technology will continue to bring further material benefits to the West, that they will permit the rest of the world to advance quickly to Western economic and technical standards, and that this process is making, in Dr Leach's phrase, men like gods,[3] with powers over their environ-

3. EDMUND LEACH, Reith Lectures for 1967. See also EMMANUEL MOUNIER, *Be Not Afraid* (La petite peur du XXe siècle) (1951), p. 70; JOHN T. MARCUS, 'Time and the Sense of History: West and East', in *Comparative Studies in Society and History*, 3 (1960–61).

ment even greater than those with which the Greeks endowed their Olympians.

Improvement, or progress, has been understood in many different senses. Since the Renaissance, few men in the West, at least, have doubted the continued progress in knowledge of the environment of man, in the natural sciences, and more recently, few have doubted the continued improvement in technology derived from them. This is the base of the pyramid of the believers in progress and includes all those who believe in progress of some kind. There are almost as many who would add that this technological improvement will also lead, in the future, to greater wealth, to an improvement in the material conditions of life, and this may be said to form the next higher, and scarcely narrower, layer of the pyramid. Those who start with the archaeological evidence would, indeed, feel more certain of progress in technology than of progress in knowledge.[4]

There would, however, be considerably fewer, and perhaps a minority only, who would feel equally persuaded that the tendency of the past, to be continued into the future, includes the improvement of social and political organization, and that human societies will become better governed, more just, freer, more equal, more stable or in other ways better equipped to permit a higher development of the human personality. This has often been believed, and some of the finest political and economic thought ever expressed may be quoted in its defence, but men are moved by experience and self-interest more than by doctrine, and there are many who would doubt whether the twentieth century was in this respect better off than the nineteenth or eighteenth, or the later decades of this century better than the earlier, and they would doubt still more whether we

4. 'The progress that archaeology can confidently detect is progress in material culture, in equipment. By its improvement human societies have with increasing success adapted themselves to their various environments and later adapted their environments to their changing needs.' V. GORDON CHILDE, *Progress and Archaeology* (1944), p. 109. Childe went on to admit that by its nature, archaeology is not well adapted to discover signs of relapse.

can be certain of continued social progress in this sense in the future.

Fewer still are those who, near the top of the pyramid, believe not only that mankind will learn more efficiently to manipulate and control its social institutions, but also that the character of man as such will change for the better, and that evolution and progress includes a humanity that will become more moral, kindlier, more cooperative, and better natured. For in this respect, little if any change has been observable in recorded history, and more faith is needed to envisage an ascent after what looks like a long plateau.

Finally, at the peak of our pyramid, there are those hopeful enough to predict that the improvements in other spheres will lead ultimately also to an improvement in the physical, mental and spiritual capacities of man, in a biological evolution that would raise future beings above man, as he has been raised above the pre-humans. They envisage an enhanced power of creation, a greater capacity to produce and enjoy works of art, and an intellect that would take the human future right out of the comprehension of the present.

The degree of optimism prevalent at any one time has fluctuated greatly in the Western world in the short span of years in which a belief in progress was widespread. At times, as during the mid-eighteenth century, when Turgot wrote his essays, or again in the decades following the triumph of Darwinism, there were many who climbed the pyramid to near its top, while at other times most men were crowded in the lower reaches. But throughout those years, few could envisage the configuration of a landscape without the safe landmark of that pyramid.

The subject has exercised many, and the literature on it is voluminous, and it is still being added to year by year. Anyone who enters this field, should be called upon to show good cause. This book attempts to make its contribution in three different ways.

First, in spite of the extent of the literature, there is no book covering the subject in a convenient length between the large and exhaustive treatment by Bury, and the epigrammatic brevity of Ginsberg. In any case, both these standard works necessarily omit the more recent contributions.

Secondly, virtually all writing on this subject consists of purely intellectual history, and derives each idea exclusively from earlier ideas, or makes, at most, passing reference to the personality and individual biography of its author. This approach, while leading to much valuable insight, ignores the fact that ideas, or at any rate those which exert any influence at all, derive from the experience, or more precisely, from the experience-in-action, of the men holding them, and the rise and fall of doctrines cannot be understood except in relation to the concrete history of their ages. This book attempts such correlation.

Finally, since the days of the polymaths of the Enlightenment of the eighteenth century, the two main groups of thinkers concerned with this body of ideas, the historian-philosophers on the one side, and the politician-economists on the other, have gone their own way, and apart from a few conscious bridge-builders, like John Stuart Mill or Marx, have scarcely glanced at each other's work. The resultant isolation has impoverished the work of both, and this volume seeks to overcome a most unnatural separation by attempting to keep the developing ideas of both in step with each other.

The idea of progress is, in this modern age, one of the most important ideas by which men live, not least because most hold it unconsciously and therefore unquestioningly. It has been called the modern religion, or the modern substitute for religion, and not unjustly so. Its character, and its assumptions, have changed with time, and so has the influence exerted by it, but at present it is riding high, affecting the social attitudes and social actions of all of us. For those who wish to know whither they are going, it may not come amiss to know something about those who helped to draw the map on which they rely.

CHAPTER ONE

THE ORIGINS OF THE
SENSE OF HISTORY

IT is a commonplace of the Western tradition that its most essential and most significant features derive from the Graeco-Roman world, from the Jewish religion as modified by early Christianity, or from the interactions of one upon the other. During the whole of the modern era, the education of countless generations, of unnumbered millions of youthful minds has been based upon this premise. Yet, curiously, the sense of history itself, including the idea of human progress, was absent in classical times, and could grow only after the mental fetters inherited from them had, at least in part, been broken.

The underlying assumptions of an age, the things commonly taken for granted to the extent that no one will bother to write them down, are not only among the most significant, but also among the most difficult to grasp by minds brought up in the thraldom of different assumptions. The modern mind cannot really conceive of a world in which man is not at the centre of the stage, and his striving after improvement not the basis of the society around him. By the same token, the Mediterranean mind of the Hellenic or Judaic world, as of other still earlier millennia, would have stood uncomprehendingly before our present worship of the idea of progress. Its victory and its dominion are modern phenomena.

Why did it elude the thinkers of antiquity? Basically, it was because it did not accord with their experience. The modern mind, extrapolating from the rapid development of its own environment, and with the benefit of the telescopic sight of centuries long ago, has no difficulty in seeing the evolution of civilized society in the one-way and irreversible, even if slow, changes of the millennia of the pre-Christian era. Among them might be the permanent settlements of formerly nomadic peoples; the creation of the empires of the river valleys with their hydraulic engineering, their mensuration and, soon, their writing; the metallurgy of bronze and iron; or the introduction and extension of slavery. But these were developments extending mostly over hundreds or thousands of years, too slow for the perception of contemporaries, though they might appear, heavily disguised, in their myths and legends. What they knew as 'history', were the day-to-day struggles of cities and empires, good and bad rulers, in which some rose and others fell, but in which there was no single sequence of change that would make historical sense. Thus the history they knew had no direction, and the history which did have direction, creating technologies, literacy, or statecraft, was out of their range of observation. If there was movement, it was downward from the golden age and from the heroes of the past.

Yet the ancients had their philosophy, their cosmogony and their religion. The Greeks, who had the advantage of standing on the shoulders of earlier highly developed Mediterranean civilizations, did consider the philosophy of an upward biological or cultural march of humanity, as they considered other possibilities, but rejected it. In line with many oriental philosophies, most Greeks held to a cyclical theory of history, in which similar situations would repeat themselves indefinitely. Others thought in terms of a fall from grace, or of totally aimless movements. Aristotelian thought precluded the idea of a change in the species itself and Platonic change, where admitted, was abrupt rather than immanent. The Epicureans, it is true, had some sense of a sequence of creation, and Lucretius' remarkable visions in *On the Nature of Things* foreshadow much modern thought, including upward stages in the uses of certain industrial materials, but these were poetic explorations at least as much as firmly based philosophic views. Seneca, comparing perhaps the glories of his age with an earlier, ruder form of society, was representative of those who held the notion of a progress of knowledge, but even he hoped for no social advantages from it, but, at best, more wisdom and greater comfort for the philosopher. In the world of the classical pagan, man's striving must be individual and internalized, he must solve the problems of living and dying for himself, rather than as a member of a growing, hopeful body of humanity.

The Judaeo-Christian world was certainly more historical than the Hellenistic world picture. Moreover, its history was no mere passage of time, but a unique drama which made sense in terms partly derived from outside itself, from the inexplicable Divine intervention in human affairs, but also partly in terms of its own happenings among historical individuals and historical nations.

The story, it is true, also begins with a fall from grace, compounded by more sinfulness thereafter. But it is due to end at a definite point in time, having run its apportioned course, and in the Christian version its uniqueness is emphasized even more by the central place taken in it by the events of a single life. The sequence of the four world empires, the Assyrian, Persian, the Greek and the Roman, each more powerful than the last, reveals a stronger sense of history than anything else known to have emerged from the East, except perhaps Zoroastrianism. Indeed, it has been claimed that

at the centre of [the Jewish] experience stands the revelation to Israel of a concept of history in terms of progress.[1]

But those who, including St Augustine, were witnesses to the fall of Rome, the last of these historic empires, thought of preparing themselves for the expected early end of the world, showing that though they might accept a sequence in the past, they did not expect to see any evolution of human society in the future, only its apocalyptic end.

For those who like to search for remote antecedents of ideas,

1. ABBA EBAN, 'The Toynbee Heresy', in M. F. Ashley Montague (ed.), *Toynbee and History* (Boston, Mass., 1956).

this Christian notion of a sequence, even if encapsuled in the narrow historic space between two eternities, may appear as an important germ of the more modern theories of development. A second component of the Augustinian philosophy which, transmuted through the centuries, was similarly destined to reappear in modern guise, was the view of history as a process with a dynamic purpose, realized essentially by the action of individuals, and according to the individual, therefore, a key role in human history. Indeed, if Mommsen's ingenious reconstruction of the intentions of Augustine's *City of God* (413–26) is correct,[2] this work is of even greater, though negative, significance in the evolution of the doctrine of human progress. According to this view, a powerful school of Christian thinkers had developed the doctrine that the mission of Christ had not only been to promise salvation for the next world, but also to increase happiness in this, the proof lying in the growing security and civilization of the Roman Empire since His coming. To Augustine, such doctrine was doubly erroneous and dangerous. On the abstract plane, it confused the absolute bliss of the Kingdom of Heaven with mundane happiness: it was the Church, not the State, which was to turn into the 'Heavenly City' of his book. On the practical plane, it made the mistake of tying Christianity too closely to the fortunes, and even the pagan totems, of worldly Rome, so that the fall of the city in 410 to heathen conquerors, notwithstanding its numerous holy places of the Church, threatened the credibility of the gospel itself. His book, the *City of God*, written to *combat* the doctrine of mundane progress, was destined to become one of the most influential sources of the philosophy of history in the Middle Ages.

Thus there was nothing in the heritage of antiquity to support the idea of human evolution and progress. Experience did not encourage the belief in an upward movement, while mythology

2. THEODOR E. MOMMSEN, 'St Augustine and the Christian Idea of Progress', *Journal of the History of Ideas* (quoted henceforth as *J. Hist. Id.*) 12 (1951).

rather suggested a decline from the golden heroic age. Those who saw man's pilgrimage as a rise from a sinful fall to ultimate grace, saw the whole of terrestrial history as merely an interlude between two forever unchanging eternities. To expand the advance of science into a general doctrine of progress would have been out of line with the ruling climate of opinion. In the end, any hope of earthly social improvement was firmly squashed by Augustine, whose views were more in accord with an empire in decay.

Much of the learning and the civilization of the classical world was transmitted to the Byzantine Empire in the East and the Muslim world in the South, rather than to the Catholic world in the North. Medieval Europe had its lasting achievements, the gradual establishment of internal security, the feudal system, a long series of technical innovations, the growth of towns and of trade and of a class of burghers, but these were scarcely evident to contemporaries, and were overshadowed in their eyes by more tangible calamities and setbacks. They could not, therefore, suggest to the Middle Ages a doctrine of permanent advance; instead, medieval man held fast to the doctrines inherited from the Old Testament, the New Testament and the Early Fathers.

If the Christian mind was more conscious than the classical of its history, and developed the concept of a meaning in history of a definite end towards which events were moving, it was at the same time also conscious of a secular decline. Nor had the rational view of history, bound up with the doctrine of progress, found much support. If there was rationality and a kind of logic in the discussions of scholars and schoolmen, the logic and the reason operated within the confines of a narrow thought structure. The outside world was still full of magic and arcane mysteries, and the decisive points in history were not those in which the laws of nature were vindicated, but those in which they were suspended; when the sun stood still, or the Red Sea defied the laws of gravity, or people were elevated up to heaven. God, who had created the world and determined its purposes, intervened actively in its running, and the purpose of man and of his history was to fulfil His commandments in the brief span of his existence within it. Only in one respect did medieval thought build a definite stepping-stone for modern thought on progress. This was the preoccupation, of thinkers ranging from Eusebius and Augustine to Otto von Freising, with the destinies of mankind as a whole, with universal, rather than local history. But these were at best preconditions, not beginnings –

The notion of progress, continual progress, with no discernible limit, on a more or less lineal ascent from an inferior condition, was unknown to mankind before the seventeenth century.[3]

It was the Renaissance which finally shattered the medieval world, and ushered in the modern age. The turning-point in European history was real, but as Michelet and Burckhardt have stressed, it was reflected also in the mind and in the spirit, in the breakthrough in thought from a static, cyclical or degenerate world into a progressive humanity.

The first expression of the belief in progress emerged out of the creation of the new science, itself the product of the newly searching, uninhibited humanism of the Renaissance, but coming into its own in the greater intellectual freedom of the seventeenth century. Science destroyed much of the old cosmology, and at the same time it became, itself, the first major aspect of human life in which men could recognize the progressive principle; science could move only one way, forward, for each generation started with the best of the last generation, and was bound to add to it. When Descartes built up a new mathematical world of confident certainty as great as that of religion, and when Newton began to encompass complex, contradictory reality itself within a few universal laws, it had become clear that

3. JOSEPH ANTHONY MAZZEO, *Renaissance and Revolution. The Remaking of European Thought* (1965, ed. of 1967), p. 275.

here was a field of endeavour in which modern man had overtaken the classics and was set on a course which would leave the
past far behind. Scientists, advancing by action rather than by
contemplation, foreshadowed the attitude of modern man. At
the same time, science and its methods were acquiring a prestige
which would lead other fields of thought to pay it the compli-
ment of imitation. Social inquiries, history itself, sought to but-
tress themselves by becoming scientific, and historians, looking
for determinate regularities which they could designate as 'laws',
were soon to light upon one for which science itself had given
the first hints: the law of human progress.

It was in astronomy that medieval pseudo-science lost some
of its first battles. But Copernicus did more than prove that it
was the earth that rotated: in the process, he also discovered the
true nature of a hypothesis, that the

fundamental principles in the form of hypotheses or assumptions
about the universe must be physically true, and incapable of being
otherwise.[4]

Copernican astronomy was matched by Leonardo's mechanics
and was duly to be followed by Galileo's physics. The voyages
of discovery opened up new continents and new riches of fauna
and flora that showed up the terrestrial ignorance of Christian
medieval Europe, and gave promise of unlimited further
treasure to be revealed.

The men of the early Renaissance could not yet embrace a
coherent philosophy of progress, since even the most optimistic
among them, who were

proud to believe that they were founding a new stage in history,

only hoped that it

would rival that of classical antiquity in brilliance, learning and
glory.

4. EDWARD GRANT, 'Late Medieval Thought, Copernicus and the
Scientific Revolution', *J. Hist. Id.* 23 (1962), p. 197.

Even this much, however, represented a 'forward movement' from the Middle Ages, which

were persuaded of the headlong decline and impending dissolution of society.[5]

As the period ran its course, some of the most sensitive thinkers, like Jean Bodin (*c.* 1530–96), who envisaged improvements in social organization, Le Roy (d. 1577), who saw his own age as superior to all others in science and the arts, and above all, Francis Bacon (1561–1626), who explicitly made the continuous and irreversible growth of scientific knowledge his engine of progress, themselves began to feel forward to the view that it was possible, and perhaps inevitable, to go beyond the achievements of the classics. After all –

a philosopher could not grasp the modern idea of progress until he realized that his own generation was superior to any yet known.[6]

It was from Bacon's *Novum Organum* (1620) that the next generations of scientists, from Descartes to Pascal, obtained the firm conviction that the 'Ancients' represented the youth of the world, while it was their own time which gloried in the accumulated wisdom of the ages. There was no need to assume that human abilities had changed over the centuries: it was just that they themselves had a larger corpus of knowledge to build upon than had earlier philosophers. Bacon's science was negating and questioning, rather than accepting, and this itself helped to undermine the awe before the great names of the past. It was as significant as it was inevitable that Bacon's historical essays, like those of his French contemporary, La Popelinière (1541–1608), should have a scientific base, discounting both miracles and

5. MARIE BOAS, *The Scientific Renaissance 1450–1630* (1962), p. 17; LORD ACTON, A Lecture on the Study of History (1895), p. 9.

6. CARL L. BECKER, *The Heavenly City of the Eighteenth-Century Philosophers* (New Haven, 1932), p. 131.

accidents, and looking instead for natural laws and causes.[7] Yet even Bacon did not believe in social progress as such, and hoped, with Plato, for a once-and-for-all lawgiver to create the ideal society as, perhaps, he also looked forward to one final discovery that would lay bare once and for all the scientific secrets of the Universe.

The seventeenth-century successors had this advantage over Francis Bacon that they could take much of the new scientific philosophy as such for granted. The century was dominated by Descartes (1596–1650), and in so far as they shared his faith in their own reasoning power, his contempt for the old shibboleths, and his quest for a total, including a social, world picture, all the scientists of the next two centuries could be said to have been Cartesian. Descartes also led them in dismissing the centuries before his own as a dark age of stagnation and expecting that the new philosophy would bring ever greater heights of achievement –

... with him, the idea of Progress takes on its full sense in the modern world.[8]

Pascal (1623–62), himself very much under Descartes' influence in his younger years, and learning from him the fruitful simile of regarding –

... the entire succession of men through the whole course of ages ... as one man, always living and incessantly learning,

brought the same optimistic organizing ability to bear on the physical world, as Descartes had to his theoretical models. The appeal was to experimentation and reason, and not to authority, and on these grounds he believed science to be progressive, for-

7. Popelinière actually recorded omens and monsters, but found natural causes for them. G. WYLIE SYPHER, 'Similarities between the Scientific and Historical Revolutions at the End of the Renaissance', *J. Hist Id.*, 26 (1965).

8. JULES DELVAILLE, *Essai sur l'histoire de l'idée de progrès jusqu'à la fin du XVIIIe siècle* (Paris, 1910), p. 178.

ever expanding into new territories, while religion (and, curiously, history also) could at best explain the same message in ever greater refinement. Pascal's optimism was exceeded by that of Leibniz (1646–1716), whose Universe was the best possible, but who nevertheless contrived to suggest that it might become better still. For man, he admitted, was less than perfect, since

the place [which] God has assigned to man in space and in time limits the perfection he was able to receive;

nevertheless

it may be even that the human race will attain in time to a greater perfection than that which we can now envisage.[9]

For Newton (1643–1727), absolute certainty extended to both his mathematical system and his physical laws, as they were both strengthening each other, and making each other inevitable. Believing in God, he felt more assured of his laws even than he did of any single experimental observation, precisely because his God was one of perfect and immutable physical laws. With Newton, who was at the height of his power in the last two decades of the seventeenth century, we reach the peak and perhaps the end of a certain development in human thought. The immense prestige imparted to physics by Newton's achievements so dominated the imagination of the next century, that other branches of inquiry, notably history, were persuaded to search for a 'scientific' base conceived in terms of simple and fundamental laws like the laws of physics. The 'laws' which historians thought to use in this way were those of the sensationalist psychology of Newton's contemporary, John Locke (1623–1704). They were to become the basis of most of the theories of progress held by the men of the Enlightenment in the eighteenth century.

It was one of the ironies of history that another contemporary,

9. LEIBNIZ, Theodicy (1710), (1952 edn), para. 341, p. 330.

Bishop Bossuet (1627–1704), as eager as Newton to defend the idea of God, chose in his *Universal History* (1681) to prove His existence not by the perfection and permanence of natural laws, as had Newton, but by the very opposite, namely, that on suitable occasions, He broke them. Bossuet's fundamentalist conservatism went against the tide which was just then rising and left him exposed to become the easy butt of Voltaire's attack, and of that of the historiography of the whole French Enlightenment, now fully committed to science and to progress.

Geology was another science which exerted a profound influence on the developing sense of history. In the hands of such intelligent practitioners as Robert Hooke or Steno, the rocks began to yield up their secrets, not only of the evolution of the earth, but also of animal and plant species preserved as fossils. Many, like Thomas Burnet, managed somehow to accommodate the whole sequence within the Biblical time scale, by making the most implausible assumptions, but it is difficult to believe that by the first half of the eighteenth century Voltaire was alone in making fun of the Biblical timespan of the world, 6,000 years according to the Vulgate, or 7,000 years according to the Septuagint. Basing himself on social history rather than on geology, and judging by the traditions of various peoples, and by a corresponding estimate of the time it would take to reach a state of civilization, Voltaire arrived at a minimum age of humanity much greater than that, and it proved difficult for his critics to attack his reasoning on this point. Pushing back the age of the earth, and with it, of humanity, not only opened up the possibility of social evolution and of progress from a more primitive state, but also weakened the oppressively narrow Christian view of history: once it was admitted that the earth had existed for millions of years before man appeared, the question of the purpose of the creation took on a new aspect.

And so, ultimately, the scene was set for fundamental advances in historiography also. One of the most significant was the changed attitude towards antiquity. In Comte's words, the idea of continuous progress had no scientific consistency, or public regard, till after the memorable controversy, at the beginning of the last [eighteenth] century, about a general comparison of the ancients and moderns.

Although the arguments in favour of the moderns were strong only in the field of science and manufacture, and much less confident in the arts, in literature, in philosophy or in general humanity, the splendours of Louis XIV's France ensured that Perrault, Terrasson and Fontenelle, the defenders of the superiority of the moderns in the 'battle of the ancients and the moderns', carried the day by about 1700. The issue was scarcely in doubt in the eighteenth century when, to quote Comte again –

. . . the human mind . . . for the first time, declared that it had made an irreversible advance.[10]

Thus the prehistory of the idea of progress ended around the close of the seventeenth century. Step by step, obstacles to its advance had been removed, its preconditions created, and finally the seeds of the idea itself had been sown. Among the obstacles were the Christian irrational view of the Universe and its doctrine of the purpose of human life, and in their place there developed, as positive preconditions, a belief in the rationality of the Universe, and the growing confidence of the power of man over his environment and, ultimately, over his destiny. There had also grown up a more scientific approach to the study of history, though this amounted as yet to little more than an honest treatment of first-hand sources and a preoccupation with the history of mankind, rather than that of a chosen people or a select society. If we take our stand on the viewpoint of the 1680s or 1690s, we discover an absolute confidence among philosophers in the progressiveness of science and technology. By contrast, hopes that society as such might progress also were, at best,

10. HARRIET MARTINEAU, *The Positive Philosophy of Auguste Comte* (2 vols., 1875); II, p. 46.

weakly expressed minority views, and it has therefore generally been held that the idea of progress first arose out of the experience of the accretion of scientific knowledge, and was centred upon that aspect of human history.

Yet to leave the story there would be to leave it incomplete and misleading. For ideas, thought systems which gain wide acceptance, though they may appear to arise solely out of the constructive adaptation of earlier ideas, do not, in fact, erupt in a vacuum. They arise in the minds of men who have experiences and social roles, and not only must they accord with those experiences and social roles, or they will be rejected, but they will arise largely because of them. That is not to say that ideas foreign to current experience may not be formed in the minds of select individuals; indeed, there is scarcely an improbability that will not occur to someone at some time. But ideas that do not accord with reality, as seen by contemporaries, will remain sterile and without influence. The new science and the idea of progress itself, both of which had widespread influence, have had their solid link with reality.

The roots of the reawakening of Europe go back a long way beyond the Renaissance. For several centuries, while Popes and Emperors fought for the attention of the world, great historic changes went on in the interstices of Western society, unnoticed, but relentlessly and irreversibly. Woods and wastes were assarted until no empty lands remained in cultivable areas, ploughs were improved, mills built, metals worked, canals dug in new ways, and innovations were made in methods of commerce and banking. This development was the product of a new type of man, as the new type of man was the product of this development. His ranks were recruited from the burghers of the newly privileged towns and guilds, the traders and fishermen and miners, and even some millers and some peasants who were immune from the worst consequences of the feudal order within a protective wall of legal privilege. These men had this in common, that they possessed the 'capitalist spirit', the 'spirit of enterprise and the desire for gain'.[11] They also fulfilled a new social role, and it is among them that we have to look for the mainspring of the mental processes behind the advances of the new science, and their concrete embodiment in new techniques. Eccentric philosophers might propound the most brilliant new hypotheses of natural philosophy; kings even might dabble in it for their pleasure, or, more commonly, in search of a method of making gold; but it was the men who had learnt in their own lives and in the business of gaining their daily bread that it was but concrete results, goods and services, unhampered by mythology which brought them success, who took the methodology of science to be a reasonable way of looking at the world and who, in turn, gave the scientists the confidence that their thinking was correct and was socially desirable, and the material backing to continue in the same direction.

That there is a connexion between rationalism and the capitalist economy and society has long been beyond dispute. Men who trade with new lands where they learn the logic of the foreigners' language, his customs, and his laws, and men who sail to new shores, are bound to feel uncomfortable under the stultifying restrictions of scholastic thought. As Catholic Europe spread into the Slav lands, pushed back the Muslim and ventured farther out to sea, there were ever larger numbers of such voyagers and traders. There might still be seekers after elixirs and philosophers' stones among the learned, but it was the engineers, who sank mines or built canals or siege engines by new principles, to whom men turned for guidance. Thus it is misleading to attribute the opening up of the new continents to the scientists with their new cosmology: on the contrary, it was traders, adventurers and mariners who persuaded the geographers that the earth was round. Science owed more to Columbus than he owed to the scientists. Once the discoveries were made, of course, the momentum of opening up the new lands, of experimenting with the new plants and foods, the influx of precious metals, set

11. WERNER SOMBART, *Quintessence of Capitalism* (1915), p. 103.

up an expansion which affected the experience within the whole of society to a point at which the idea of progress could be widely accepted as reasonable.

Quite apart from the great discoveries, much of the science of the Renaissance itself arose, not in secluded laboratories, but in the workshops of artisans and craftsmen, in which particularly the idea of scientific cooperation, and of scientific progress for the sake of science, or for the glory of the country, first arose –

Manifestly, the idea of science we usually regard as Baconian is rooted in the requirements of early capitalist economy and technology: its rudiments appear first in the treatises of fifteenth-century craftsmen.[12]

Many of the other key ideas of the Renaissance were first debated centuries earlier in the centres of capitalist commerce, especially in Paris and the cities of Northern Italy, and such men as Bacon, Rabelais, Le Roy or Bodin caught their first glimpses of the idea of progress when they observed the tangible proofs of compasses, printing, gunpowder, and the other by-products of the capitalist expansion of their day.

Again, the advance of science in the face of organized religion was not simply the result of the sudden superiority of scientific thought or of a sudden growth of Christian tolerance. On the contrary, the skill and enthusiasm of the Churches for murdering their heretical opponents were, if anything, greater in the sixteenth and seventeenth centuries than they had been before, fanned as they were by the Reformation and the Counter-

---

12. EDGAR ZILSEL, 'Genesis of the Idea of Scientific Progress', *J. Hist. Id.*, 6 (1945), p. 346; also his 'The Sociological Roots of Science', *Amer. Journal of Sociology*, 47 (1943); GIORGIO DE SANTILLANA, 'The Role of Art in the Scientific Renaissance', in M. Clagett (ed.), *Critical Problems in the History of Science* (Madison, 1959). This emphasis is to some extent criticized by RUPERT HALL, 'The Scholar and the Craftsman in the Scientific Revolution', ibid. These two paper as well as the paper by M. E. Prior quoted above, are reprinted in L. R. MARSAK, *The Rise of Science in Relation to Society* (New York, 1964).

Reformation. The comparative safety of the scientist became assured only when a substantial number of the powerful and the rich began to find his ideas inherently reasonable and promising. In turn, the new middle classes might, like the merchant of Prato, still fear for their immortal souls if they concentrated too much on the affairs of this world; but in practice, such ideas were pushed into the back of their minds in the process of living and striving as merchants, and became little more than occasional twinges of conscience. This was part of the process analysed in the great debate on Religion and the Rise of Capitalism. What has emerged most significantly at the end of the debate is not only the wide range over which Protestant ideas coincided with the needs of the new capitalist class, but also the extent to which Catholic doctrine was modified in the same direction.

Thus it was the New Men of Europe, the merchants and traders and manufacturers, the owners of mines and mills and of banks, and their technicians and managers and doctors and clerks, whose experience tallied with the new philosophy, and whose needs called forth the new science. They had little regard for the privileges of birth or for divine rights, but required instead rewards for merit, freedom of contract, protection of property and defencelessness of labour, and in the end they won, for their economy was the more efficient. In the two or three centuries before the 1680s or 1690s, their advance and the growing acceptance of their values were sufficiently marked to make a doctrine of progress seem plausible to them. When they made their bid for power against a well entrenched landed class system which used tradition as its ideology, they would find the slogan of Progress most useful, while those in North America found it even more natural. The idea of progress will be much misunderstood unless it is viewed as playing its role within the real, concrete history of the men who held it.

CHAPTER TWO

THE CENTURY OF THE ENLIGHTENMENT

THE eighteenth century, which saw the first wave of optimism about the destiny of mankind, also saw it reach its highest point. It opened with a fair degree of agreement on progress in one field only: science and technology. Before its close, firm convictions had been expressed about the inevitability of progress in wealth, in civilization, in social organization, in art and literature, even in human nature and biological make-up. But the century ended in the explosion of the French Revolution, which shattered again the hopes particularly of those who had hoped the most.

In that century, the main scene of action was France, with Scotland as a secondary focus. 'It is', it has been observed,

practically impossible to judge, even to grasp the ideologies of progress unless one studies the environment which has nourished them, and considers their social and human characteristics.[1]

On the whole, the *philosophes* who battled with great fervour and an enviable range of knowledge in the field of history, science, politics, economics or philosophy for their vision of the Enlightenment, were personally disinterested men, fighting for the sake of what they saw as truth and humanity. Nevertheless, it would be idle to pretend that this was a purely intellectual battle, fought without social purposes: the conviction of righteousness, the impatience, the daily practical examples of their doctrines, came to the *philosophes* from the experience of the French bourgeois whom they, consciously or unconsciously, represented. It was he who saw endless possibilities of wealth, of power, of social approval, of genuine betterment for his society – if only the restrictions and murderous taxation of the State, the

1. GEORGES FRIEDMANN, *La Crise du progrès. Esquisse d'histoire des idées 1895–1935* (Paris, 2nd edn 1936), p. 11.

idle extravagance of the nobility or the privileged dead hand of the Church did not hold him back. They genuinely followed a vision of justice and truth, but it was justice and truth as seen by the bourgeois.

Nothing is more instructive than to observe the differences between the doctrines on history, politics and economics as expounded by English, Scots and Dutch authors on the one hand, and those of the French or Italians on the other. They breathe the same intellectual atmosphere, and they all seek after absolute and eternal truths, but the first group write from positions of strength, with their main demands fairly met, and the second from without the gates, underprivileged, and still engaged in preparing themselves to assault the fortress. In all these countries capitalism itself was an undoubted and patently progressive force, but what was conservative in Britain, was subversive in France, and this was the basic reason for the dichotomy between what was and what ought to be, between experience and reason, in French thought. The vision of progress of the eighteenth century is essentially the *bourgeois* vision of progress.

The French Enlightenment ranged over the whole field of intellectual endeavour: the *encyclopédie* became its most enduring monument. But the idea of progress, which permeated all the leading luminaries, the *philosophes,* though in different forms and to different degrees, is basically a view of history, and we must therefore begin with some comments on the historiography of the age.

Like much else, it was conceived in reaction to what had gone before. The principles of writing history hitherto, it was felt, had been mistaken, bigoted, limited in range, blinkered, and biased. Instead, history too should be bathed in the light of reason. It should make sense, that is to say, it should subject itself to analysis, and it should be didactic, or, in Bolingbroke's oft-quoted phrase, it should be 'philosophy teaching by example'.[2] In the

2. VISCOUNT BOLINGBROKE (1678–1751), *Letters on the Study and Use of History* (1799 edn), p. 14.

nature of the case, it was likely to show little beyond the cruelties and follies of former ages, before the dawning of the age of reason.

This posture was somewhat negative, but it led to new and fruitful approaches. Thus the European Middle Ages, representing indirectly the autocracy, the feudal privileges and the irrationality of the Church against which the Enlightenment was currently battling, were treated with sharp hostility and contempt. To emphasize this point, the achievements of other, non-Christian contemporary societies, such as Islam or the Chinese civilization, were studied and sometimes praised much beyond their deserts. But genuine 'universal' history (unlike Bossuet's, which was misnamed and was limited to Christendom) could be used to illustrate and evolve the picture of a single human historical evolution –

For the men of the Enlightenment the idea of world-history was particularly congenial. It fitted in with their notion of progress, their view of mankind, advancing steadily from primitive barbarism to reason and virtue and civilization.[3]

Thus in Voltaire's *Essai sur les Moeurs et l'Esprit des Nations* (1756), or in Adam Ferguson's *Essay on the History of Civil Society* (1767) these excursions become the basis of an embryonic historical sociology. Similarly, the massive treatment given by Gibbon in his *Decline and Fall* (1776–88) to the barbarians as well as the Romans changed irreversibly the whole course of classical studies.

The contempt for kings and priests changed the emphasis from reigns, battles, and religious controversies, to general cultural and social, and at times even economic, history. This had the superficial attraction of giving greater historical significance

3. G. BARRACLOUGH, 'Universal History', in H. P. R. Finberg (ed.), *Approaches to History* (1962), p. 84; also T. J. G. LOCKER, *Die Überwindung des europäozentrischen Geschichtsbildes* (1954).

to the actions of the bourgeoisie; but on a deeper level, it permitted for the first time a genuinely rational, systematic treatment of historical evolution.

At first, the interest centred largely on cultural history, on the development of science, of rational views, and of laws, but this quickly extended to more concrete social facts.

What I should like to know is the sort of society then in existence, how men lived in the interior of their families, what arts were practised,

Voltaire exclaimed in his *Moeurs*, and he criticized Puffendorf for having excluded the

forces of the country, how well the people fed, how the people of Gothland are joint to those who ravaged the Roman Empire, how the arts were introduced with the passage of time in Sweden, what are her main laws, her wealth, or her poverty.[4]

But this list is as remarkable for its omissions as for its inclusions, and in his main historical work, the *Siècle de Louis XIV* (1751), his chapters on these topics are very short. Hume (1711–76), in his *History of England* (1754–61) declared it desirable to

take a general survey of the age, so far as regards manners, finances, arms, commerce, arts and sciences. The chief use of history is that it affords materials for disquisitions of this nature.

A. F. Tytler, (1747–1813), a fellow Scotsman, in his *Plan and Outline of ... Universal History* (1782), echoed these views –

It is necessary to bestow attention particularly on the manners of nations, their laws, the nature of their government, their religion, their intellectual improvements, and progress in the arts and sciences.

More precisely, William Robertson, (1721–93), yet another Scot,

4. J. H. BRUMFITT, *Voltaire: Historian* (1958), chapter 3: Social History, also p. 160; J. B. BLACK, *The Art of History* (1926), pp. 34–6.

has enough of the enlightenment within him to see in science and trade the most powerful levers for progress.[5]

The contrast with the traditional school was still great in Arthur Young's time (1741–1820). In 1788 he wrote that

reading modern history is generally the most tormenting employment that a man can have: one is plagued with the actions of a detestable set of men called conquerors, heroes, and great generals; and we wade through pages loaded with military detail; but when you want to know the progress of agriculture, of commerce, and industry, their effect in different ages and nations on each other – the wealth that resulted – the division of that wealth – its employment – and the manners it produced – all is blank. Voltaire set an example, but how has it been followed.[6]

In addition to its interest in universal, and in economic and social history, a third product of the new trend in eighteenth-century historiography was the idea of historical states. These were not to be thought of as simple accidental sequences, but to be logically and scientifically connected, so that each arose necessarily and inherently out of the preceding one, and contained within itself the inescapable seeds of the one following. It is evident that if we were to add to this the conviction that each stage was, in some sense, 'superior' to the last, we would arrive at the complete idea of progress.

Curiously, the earliest and, in some way, most strikingly modern version of the stage theory did not assume an upward movement, but envisaged a cycle of rise and decline, of a *corso e ricorso* in the life of each 'nation'. Giambattista Vico's (1668–1744) *Scienza Nuova* (1725, revised 1730) developed out of the

5. MEINECKE, *Die Enstehung des Historismus*, (Munich, 1959, 1st edn 1946), p. 239; J. R. HALE, *The Evolution of British Historiography* (1967, 1st edn 1964), pp. 150, 163–4; T. P. PEARDON, *The Transition in English Historical Writing 1760–1830* (New York, 1966, 1st edn 1933), p. 62.

6. Quoted in HALE, p. 35.

mental climate of the Italian 'academies', by then somewhat outside the mainstream of European culture, but remained unknown in its own century, though Montesquieu seems to have had access to it, and it was rediscovered by an admiring Michelet a hundred years after its first appearance. Vico believed that there was a pattern, or

ideal eternal history traversed in time by the history of every nation in its rise, progress, maturity, decline and fall,

the main stages being the divine or religious period, the heroic or mythical, and the civil, scientific, reasonable or adult phase. In sharp distinction with the later philosophers, Vico was certain of his 'axioms' precisely because

the world of civil society has certainly been made by men, and that its principles are therefore to be found within the modifications of our own human mind

like Geometry, for example, but unlike Physics which describes the world made by God. Moreover –

wherever the same circumstances are present, the same phenomena arise and no others,

and in the social field it is the selfish actions of untold numbers of individuals which inevitably collaborate to produce a predicted result –

human choice, by its nature most uncertain, is made certain and determined by the common sense of men with respect to human needs or utilities.

Vico is thus the forerunner of all those who hold to a determinist scientific history, based on social 'laws' of evolution which ensure a single pattern of development. His scheme is cyclical, but not totally unprogressive. For the beginnings of humanity (not merely of each national life cycle) –

... in the nature of things, must ... have been small, crude and quite obscure

compared with the present

enlightened, cultivated and magnificent times,

and European nations, being Christian, are thereby more civilized than earlier barbarian nations were at a similar stage of the cycle.[7]

In many respects it is but a short step from Vico the outsider, to Montesquieu (1689–1755), one of the central and most significant figures of the Enlightenment. Montesquieu, too, believed in the existence of natural 'laws' relating to social and historical behaviour, though he would not have endorsed Vico's belief that they were easier to discover than those of the physical sciences. One main aim of his greatest work, *De l'Esprit des lois* (1748) was to trace the relationship between man made legal systems, and the inescapable laws of nature. For Montesquieu, the latter were primary, and our power, as sentient beings, of making choices depended on the use of our reason and our understanding of natural laws. Historical necessity is always stronger than individual –

If Caesar and Pompey had thought like Cato, others would have thought like Caesar and Pompey; and the republic, destined to perish, would have been dragged to the precipice by another hand.

Again –

it is not chance that rules the world ... there are general causes, moral and physical, which act in every monarchy elevating it, maintaining it, or hurling it to the ground. All accidents are controlled by these causes. And if the chance of one battle – that is, a particular cause – has brought a state to ruin, some general cause

7. Quotations from *The New Science of Giambattista Vico* (translated by T. G. Bergin and M. H. Fish), (Ithaca, N.Y., 1948), paras. 123, 141, 144, 147, 331 and 349. No. 147 is in Edmund Wilson's translation from Michelet's French, as the Bergin and Fish version, never very lucid, is virtually incomprehensible.

made it necessary for that state to perish from a single battle. In a word, the main trend draws with it all particular accidents.[8]

It was Montesquieu's intention to disentangle the permanent features of a historical situation from the variable effects of the human will.

The core of his philosophy of history was sociological. What he attempted was a theory of social development, based on what he would today call 'ideal types' to which he allowed an unusually wide range of influence –

The political and civil laws [he stated] should be in relation to the climate of each country, to the quality of its soil, to its situation and extent, to the principal occupation of the natives, whether husbandmen, huntsmen, or shepherds: they should have relation to the degree of liberty which the constitution will bear; to the religion of the inhabitants, to their inclinations, riches, numbers, commerce, manners, and customs.[9]

This historical relativism, or historicism, implied in the emphasis on existing 'manners and customs' as well as on economic relationships, gave Montesquieu his built-in development theory for an inherent, analytically provable historical progress. Unlike most other authors of the Enlightenment, he would, if hard pressed, give preference to the 'irrational', or naturalistic view, as on the issue of slavery, which from a rational point of view was simply wrong, but appeared much more justifiable if viewed in relation to such empirical considerations as climate, agriculture, technique, and existing manners.

It is therefore particularly unjustified to fasten on Montesquieu the epithet of being 'unhistorical', of ignoring past history for a rational ideal. Essentially it is unfair to his associates also, for it was their wish to improve society which set them studying

8. MONTESQUIEU, *Considerations on the Causes of the Greatness of the Romans and their Decline* (1734, revised 1748), translated by David Lowenthal (New York, 1965), pp. 108, 169.

9. MONTESQUIEU, *The Spirit of Laws* (1748), translated by Th. Nugent (London, 2 vols. 1878), I, 7.

history, and they studied history in order to establish the laws of social change.

The basic ambiguity of the Enlightenment view of history thus emerges clearly in Montesquieu. One extreme was developed by Justus von Möser (1720–94), who, stressing the irrationality of concrete events, picked on Montesquieu's concept of the 'spirit of the age', 'total impression' and the need for an *Einleben und Einfühlen in die Dinge,* instead of a scientific analysis. This, coupled with his sense of historical sequence, appears recognizably in the German idealist philosophy by the end of the century. At the other extreme, the appeal to the constancy of human nature, and the importance of climate, reappears in such positive sociology as that of Adam Ferguson (1723–1816). Montesquieu's ambiguity extended also to the idea of progress. He had no doubt that the past ages were more barbarous, that there had been an improvement to his own age, and that there were certain reforms necessary in order to adapt civil law to the natural laws then operating in France. But it is far less clear that he had any thought of continuous progress beyond a generalized hope from the rule of reason.

The scientists and *philosophes* who produced the encyclopédie, and their forerunners, were conscious of two major influences behind their belief in progress. One was the visible advance of science and technology which, encouraged by the needs of society, had 'taken off' and become airborne with a momentum which appeared to be all their own. The other was the Lockean philosophy and psychology, dominating the embryonic social sciences of the eighteenth century as Newton dominated the physical ones. For Locke (1632–1704), particularly in his *Essay Concerning Human Understanding* (1690), had removed innate sin and depravity and put in their place the idea that man, by the plasticity of his nature, could be brought into harmony with a harmonious natural world around him. The gnawing question about the existence of evil which is that it must be permitted by God, yet must also be natural, was answered by the most optimistic thought of all, that the world was as yet unfinished, but could be perfected. Locke also provided the link with political reality, for his ideal of the Constitutional State, providing liberty and security, particularly of contracts and of property, was a description of Britain and therefore a realistic target for the French bourgeoisie.

But these two sets of ideas were fundamentally contradictory, and any philosophy based on them was bound to be ambiguous or inconsistent. In the social and political field, the *philosophes* whose historical thinking was in terms of ideas, knowledge and 'manners', rather than material benefits, and those who themselves had little need for more wealth failed to see any possibility of improving on a rational social system based on perfect reason and justice: Locke's own social contract implies a fixed, rather than a progressive society. Thus there arose from the beginning a conservative wing, with its social base among the enlightened nobility and the wealthier merchants and manufacturers.

By contrast with finite social development, natural science offered a vista of unbroken advance –

The one great conception which belongs to this [positive] third phase [noted Comte] is that of human progress, as an express view. It could only arise from the scientific evolution as a whole . . . Pascal, who first expressed the philosophical conception of human progress . . . certainly derived it from the general history of mathematical sciences.

This generalization, Comte added shrewdly, was upheld by

the evident conformity between scientific and industrial progression.[10]

From Pascal, the line runs via Bayle and Fontenelle to Diderot and his colleagues. Pierre Bayle (1647–1706) used the prestige of science to raise the standing of history. Fontenelle discovered

10. MARTINEAU, op. cit., pp. 356–7. Comte believed that there was a similar progression in the aesthetic field.

the progressive dynamics of physical science, creating in its devotees a sense of mission and a dedication to pure research for the benefit of mankind, and allowing them at the same time to learn from the past and to be liberated from it. He became perhaps the first to see science as inherently progressive, unlike poetry, by constantly adding to the stock of knowledge, and by being consciously self-critical. If the Middle Ages were treated as a temporary aberration, scientific progress could be seen to have been the rule for the whole of known human history. None of this assumed change in individual human capacities, which obeyed the law of the uniformity of nature –

If we had been put in the place of [the ancients], we should have made their inventions; if they had been put in ours, they would have added to what they would have found invented already.[11]

As you could not add to the capacity of society as a whole, there was no room here for general social historical progress outside science.

There was, however, one more optimistic strand of thought, which believed in infinite social and political progress. It was best represented by Saint-Pierre. The Abbé de Saint-Pierre (1658–1743), a Cartesian, deist, and rationalist, yielded to no one in his optimism about the possibilities of science, but he had a much stronger awareness of social reality than most of his contemporaries. Scientific advances occurred not merely because of the genius of the scientists, but because of the invention of printing, the rise of the Academies, and the growth of leisure, and these in turn were built on the solid foundations of the new commerce and the new wealth. The Iron Age had been followed by the Bronze Age and the (present) Silver Age; isolated man advanced to organization by families, tribes and ultimately states regulated by constitutions. Yet, so far, social and particularly moral and political progress had been minimal, and he urged the philosophers to devote themselves to that

11. FONTENELLE, *Oeuvres* (Paris, 1766 edn), IV, 175.

cause, certain that in the light of reason they could solve the outstanding problems there within a century, to inaugurate the golden age. His writings contain the first consistent statement of the utilitarian principle of the greatest happiness of the greatest number, derived from his humanism and based, unlike that of his nineteenth-century successors, on the conviction that the State and its laws had it in their power to mould the morals of peoples. He himself proposed schemes for a European peace organization, a Moral Academy and professors of politics, which have earned him much ridicule since; but he was author of two of the most important later extensions of the idea of progress: continuous improvement in social and political organization and behaviour and, even more optimistically, continuous improvement in the morals of humanity.

The first great upsurge of the belief in reason culminated in the work of the encyclopedists. Voltaire had visited England in 1726 and his *Letters from England* which appeared in England in 1733 and in France in 1734 exalted Locke, Newton and English political freedom. The great *encyclopédie* arose out of a project to edit a French version of Chambers's encyclopedia of 1728. The example of England and the favoured position of her bourgeoisie were therefore near the heart of the French Enlightenment. Its high point, coinciding with a certain relaxation of the oppressiveness of the *ancien régime*, fell in the years *c.* 1751–65.

Basically, the encyclopedists saw themselves as scientists. If many held the faith in progress as a kind of religion, and Tawney has suggested that 'Age of Faith' would be a better description than the 'Age of Reason', they worshipped God or the Supreme Being only because of the perfection of nature and its laws which were being revealed by their discoveries. Nature became the clock, from which one argued back to the clockmaker, and apart from nature, they would, like the Revolution later, be prepared to worship at the altar of the 'Goddess of Reason'. But even if they were all scientists, it must be a matter of some surprise that so many of the leading luminaries of the age could be found to agree sufficiently in their, for the time, rather dangerous and extremist politics, as to take on indifferently articles for the encyclopedia on the natural sciences as well as on legal, political and philosophical questions, which would yet produce at the end a cohesive whole.

What gave them their ideological unity? Of course, they had in common their rationalism, their Descartes, Newton and Locke; but beyond these they also had their economic interests. The relationship between the concrete demands of a class in an actual historical situation, its sometimes violent struggles to achieve them, and the parallel development of internally consistent doctrines derived from preceding doctrines, many of which had nothing directly to do with politics, is exceedingly complex. Yet it is not too difficult to see the source of the axioms of the Enlightenment: equality of rights and equality before the law, for instance, though not equality of property rights; freedom of political expression, at least for the educated; the right to trade freely or to choose one's profession freely, with rewards in proportion to merit; and above all, security of person and property from the arbitrary action of the Prince. In all this, the success of Britain served as focus. Moreover, as is the rule in these cases, the immediate demands were inevitably elevated into eternal principles.

Political demands and descriptive natural sciences were one thing, but descriptive social science was quite another, for the authors had no experience of a free capitalist economy under the *ancien régime*. They had to imagine one, and at the same time attempt to justify their preference for it; they were still polemicizing rather than describing. In consequence, their political economy was stultified as Physiocracy, and the science was developed wholly in Britain. It is not without significance that the first generalized description of the economy to emerge out of France was (like Law's Mississippi Scheme of 1719–20) the brainchild of a Briton, Richard Cantillon (c. 1680–1734). French sociology and social psychology similarly suffered from the fact that the ideal rational society still lay in the future, while current studies still ran the danger of censorship and persecution.

The result was that the social science of the Enlightenment became solidly based on history. Religious beliefs, moral and judicial ideas, language, institutions, were all explained by their development, and the *philosophes* were therefore deeply conscious of history and of historical progress up to their own times. Yet their psychology, as transmitted from Locke and developed by Condillac (1715–80), did not allow any change in human nature; thus their observed social changes had to come from outside the individual, from historical developments in society. With the duality of fixed, eternal laws on the one hand, played out against a shifting scenery of concrete historical social situations on the other, we have therefore reached the threshold of a complete theory of progress.

Condillac took from Locke not merely the idea of an unchanging capacity of the individual, but also the idea that our minds would be acted upon by our environment, while we, in turn, could act upon our environment, if we understood its laws, which also included the laws of human behaviour. Since the human mind was improvable, there was thus the potential here for a virtuous, upward spiral, the minds of each generation being improved by the improved conditions created by their predecessors, and in turn, as a consequence of this better start, being enabled to make the conditions still better for the next generation, without any enlarged biological capacity. This potential upward impulse would work because the world, like the human mind, was rational and would respond positively to rational human action. As he stressed particularly in his *Traité des Systèmes*, the principles of the physical universe and the principles on which the mind operated were identical.

The same point was also made by D'Alembert (1717–83), particularly in his *Discours Préliminaire*, the introduction to the first volume of the encyclopedia. Basing himself on the advances made by Newton, he believed that scientific progress would lead to an ever smaller number of laws of growing applicability, until the whole of knowledge would be encompassed by a single set of laws and a single science. For D'Alembert, a brilliant mathematician, science was perhaps a more dominant driving force for progress than for most of the other *philosophes*, and it is therefore all the more curious that he should visualize the impulses behind this force to consist of new ideas hitting individual thinkers somewhat haphazardly, rather than with a socially conditioned inevitability.

The other leading belief of Condillac, of the omnipotence of the environment, became the basis of the social philosophy also of Helvétius (1715–71); his work *De l'Esprit* (1758), in which he attempted to prove that the sensations which the mind received from outside were the source of all intellectual activity, had the distinction of being denounced by the Sorbonne and publicly burned after condemnation by the Parliament of Paris, so that it enjoyed a particularly wide fame and large readership. He was convinced that, given a rational education, there was no limit set to the progress of humanity to become 'happy and powerful'.

Helvétius also developed St Pierre's utilitarian principle of the greatest happiness of the greatest number, to the point at which it was taken over by Bentham for his own detailed blueprints for social engineering. This principle was basically mathematical, and with its aid the work of the lawgiver could be reduced to the simplicity of a calculus. He could dole out incentives of pleasure and pain, to produce desirable social results like an intelligent schoolmaster in a class of schoolchildren. There was thus an authoritarian streak in Helvétius' philosophy, of the kind to reappear again and again in the thought systems of all the planners and all the philanthropists. But in his case the authority lay in the system rather than the lawgiver for, if the right facts and quantities were fed into it, the correct measures would emerge of themselves, and Government would be merely an instrument. Besides, the calculus also showed that the best results would be achieved in a democratic system.

History had already shown her benevolence in other ways. Science had brought benefits to humanity by ending the reign of old superstitions that had diminished human happiness, and it had helped to prolong human life. Commercial expansion and geographical discoveries had opened up sources of wealth which had benefited some and could be made to benefit all. The rise of civilization, the development from the barbarism of primitive hunting societies, to the more advanced stages of pastoral communities, to settled agriculture, and to the civilization such as was enjoyed by the France of the eighteenth century, were not accidental. Each stage saw less unhappiness, and more happiness, than the preceding one; for in opposition to Rousseau, Helvétius did not believe that primitive man was either happier, gentler or more virtuous than his civilized successor. On the contrary, since knowledge of the truth will make men more virtuous, as greater physical comfort and security will make them gentler and happier, history is the record of the increase of human happiness. There is, however, a deeper and analytically more satisfying reason for the conviction that the sequence of social stages was no accident: the evolution of modern society was the product of human volition, and all past history is the result of man's search for happiness and avoidance of unhappiness. To perpetuate unhappiness when known methods of its avoidance existed would not only be irrational, but would also be 'unnatural', and therefore was out of the question when viewing past events.

We arrive back, therefore, at the link between knowledge and the increase in happiness. Society and its rulers are increasingly able, because of greater knowledge, to combine the individual with the general interest, and the laws of nations will increasingly be changed to increase both. Thus the undoubted future progress of the human spirit will be accompanied by continuous social and individual amelioration.

Helvétius was, in point of fact, a considerably finer and more discriminating social thinker and historian than some of the cruder British Utilitarians who lived two or three generations after him, and who were unable to envisage, except in the shape of caricature, a society with terms and values other than their own brash capitalism. He was not convinced, for example, that beyond a certain point of health and comfort, the simple amassing of wealth would promote greater happiness, but on the contrary, assumed that an increasingly wise society will withdraw from the rat race for ever larger fortunes, and learn contentment in domestic occupations, in tilling its land and engaging in trade only for necessities. Neither did he avoid the further dilemma facing the Utilitarians that, at any given period, the redistribution of wealth from the rich to the poor would very greatly increase the happiness to be derived from that wealth. However, though aware of the evils created by large fortunes, he did not believe in equality. Besides –

The preservation of private property is the moral God of the State.[12]

Helvétius might be called a philanthropist, but he was a bourgeois philanthropist, after all.

Another Utilitarian was the Marquis de Chastellux (1734–88), whose *Félicité Publique* appeared in 1772. Though not to be counted among the encyclopedists, he was sufficiently close to them in outlook to receive a mention here. He believed that future legislators, unlike those of the past, would have their efforts –

... directed to that sole end of all governments, the *acquisition of the greatest welfare of the greatest number of individuals*.

Planning the happiness of others would by itself make men happier, and the sum total of happiness would be enlarged by an increase in population –

12. HELVETIUS, *De l'Homme* (posth. 1772), Sect. X, Ch. 8.

All which tends to multiply men within the nations, and rich crops, over the surface of the earth, is good in itself.

Better still was an increase of food production faster than population, such as had already taken place in England. This was 'the surest sign of the felicity of mankind'.[13]

The Baron D'Holbach (1723–89) was equally optimistic about the conjoint progress of science, material comforts, education and human happiness. The most thoroughgoing materialist among the *philosophes* of the French Enlightenment, he was unwilling, in his *Système de la Nature* (1770) to tolerate even the compromise of a 'Supreme Being' proposed by his contemporaries. Nor did he, as a good materialist, envisage any state of perfect bliss in the future: all possible progress would be slow and painful, and it would be led by philosophers who were only one step ahead of the pack. The general direction, however, was clear. Ignorance had been the principal evil, and now that we knew how to organize society so as to harmonize everyone's interest with a growth of sympathy, understanding and affection among members of society, we could look forward to continuous improvement. Social collaboration itself, leading to division of labour, to inequality, to exchange, would increase happiness, *pari passu* with making Government more virtuous, because better educated, and political life more moral.

The editor of the encyclopedia, Diderot (1713–84), had felt the oppression of the *ancien régime* more than most, not only by having his first major work, *Pensées Philosophiques* (1746) burnt by order of the Parliament of Paris, but by being imprisoned for three months in 1749 for another tract, *Lettre sur les Aveugles*, which attempted to show that human mental processes derived from the impressions of the senses. Yet he was, at the same time, the least dogmatic among the encyclopedists. It may be that his flexibility, his greater willingness to admit exceptions and imperfections, was not unconnected with the fact

13. F. J. DE CHASTELLUX, *An Essay on Public Happiness* (English edn of 1790, 2 vols.), II, 112, 256, 375–6.

that his main scientific interests were in the field of biology rather than physics.

His biological studies of different species had convinced him both of the regularity and conformity to law of all the physical universe, and of the uniqueness of life. Applied to evolution, this became the 'transformism', that is the twin principle of change and continuity, that brilliantly anticipated the later Lamarckian and Darwinian ideas of evolution, as well as much modern thought on the philosophy of history. It was this principle, applied to human history, which proved that nature 'wanted' man to be improved, and signs of this were to be seen in the rise of the sciences and, particularly, of the applied sciences, for which he proposed the foundation of an Academy of the mechanical arts.

But Diderot was impressed much more by facts than by systems of thought, and while the analogy with nature gave him the conviction of individual human perfectibility, it did not entirely remove his scepticism regarding social improvement, that is the improvement of the social arrangements. He had no doubt that civilization was capable of progress, but he had, like Rousseau, much admiration for the noble savage, and voiced much criticism of the corrupting luxury of modern Europe. He was certain of evolution, but no more than hopeful of future human progress.

The astonishingly wide area of agreement among such a large group of talented, thoughtful people as the encyclopedists together with other leading contemporaries like Voltaire, Montesquieu, Turgot and even Rousseau, has no parallel in history until the arrival of the modern Marxist movement. The reasons for both are not dissimilar. For the *philosophes* of the Enlightenment were, as it were, fully agreed at both ends of their thought spectrum. At the purely intellectual extreme the inescapable foundation of their thought was the emergence of science, expanding and accelerating upon its expansion as the avalanche of new facts and new theories brought ever more aspects of knowledge within its orbit. At the other, practical extreme, they were all united in the politico-economic demands of the French bourgeoisie which, by the mid-century, had a sharp, well-defined focus: the rights and liberties of England, to which were soon to be added those of the United States.

They also, and for much the same reason, shared an irrepressible optimism as to the future of their society, if governed by science and reason – an optimism not yet diluted by any actual experience of government and of turning principles into legislative enactments. They agreed fairly closely in their contempt for the past; they agreed that their own age had reached a level of civilization and 'manners' higher than anything that had ever been seen before; and there was no sign of a reversal – on the contrary, the scientific method would ensure that their common ideal of a good society would soon be brought about. The line connecting these three reference points of past, present and future was the foundation line of their theory of progress. There was no agreement on the shape of the extrapolation, but the mental picture of human history was, ineradicably, an upward-sloping curve.

The distance between scientific rationalism and the bourgeois liberal ideal, covered by slightly varying routes by the different members of the school, was also traversed by a direct underground cable. For the capitalist world was a rationalist world in principle, in stark contrast to feudal and priest-ridden societies. Decisions in merchants' counting houses are made by a rational calculus and the results can be mathematically tested by a profit rate. In the ideal capitalist world, success goes to merit, for all start equal before the law, and will flourish only as they satisfy human needs. Privilege, caprice, coercion and restriction, the principles of French economic life in the mid-eighteenth century, were as much in conflict with rational thought as with the fortunes of the ambitious bourgeois.

The belief in natural harmony, in the benevolence of nature or in kindly and rational humanity was only apparently contradicted by their account of earlier times, and of the Middle Ages in particular. The new, progressive element that had been lacking in the past was knowledge, and for that lack, the past had become a plaything of barbarism and irrationality, despite human instinct to the contrary. Their generation had for the first time achieved the power that comes with knowledge.

At its lowest level, they could now visualize some superior lawgiver able to manipulate the social units so as to direct human impulses, good and bad, to socially desirable ends. This was essentially to be the basis of the new political economy evolved in Scotland. Reason here becomes knowledge, technique, and the individual is the object, rather than the subject, of its exercise. Moreover, it might lead, not to a continuously upward path of progress, but to a high plateau, a consummation, from which there can be no further ascent.

But there was a higher level, too. Their end, as philosophers, was so to set the scene by legislation as to allow the maximum freedom of action to individuals. Individuals would know their own interests best, and freedom would thus ensure the fastest growth of happiness. In turn, the achievement of this end of greater happiness, which is another definition of 'progress', was the sole justification for the State, and the implied social contract that lies behind it. The State was the servant of the individual. The implied or open placing of the individual in the centre of the picture was to prove among the most revolutionary thoughts of the Enlightenment.

The indebtedness of the encyclopedists to Locke, and to the English experience which he summarized so brilliantly, is therefore clear; but the indebtedness also extended further, to his sensationalist doctrine of knowledge. All the *philosophes* agreed on the influence of experience and sensations, and therefore on the power of education, and for each of them education, rather than revolution, was to be the key to the better, rational society. Even if it deliberately excluded what was known to Diderot and others about heredity and stability in the species, it was, in principle, one of the most powerful engines of progress and of the idea of progress, explaining at one and the same time the failures of the past and the promise of the future.

In one major respect, therefore, the adverse judgement on the Enlightenment, particularly common in the nineteenth century, that it was 'unhistorical', was false. Not only did the leading authors of the French Enlightenment do a great deal to further genuine historical studies and to free historiography from its concentration on Europe and on politico-military matters, as well as from the surviving practices of treating religious miracles on the same terms as more rationally credible events; what is more to the point, the whole basis of their sociological theories was historical. They set out to provide an account and an explanation of change. All of them began with the conviction that their own age was different from any that had gone before, and this was near the heart of their philosophy, in the form of the doctrine of progress.

Yet there is some substance in the criticism. For most of the *savants* of the Enlightenment wished to turn history into a science like astronomy or physics. They looked for man-in-general, for eternally valid truths about society and for vast universal systems. But in practice their theory and their 'facts' inevitably sprang largely from their own experience. Thus all previous ages were judged by the standards of French eighteenth-century civilization and the histories written by the group showed a singular lack of understanding of earlier societies, which they were inclined to regard largely as characterized by barbarism, superstition and hateful aberrations best forgotten.

Moreover, they also held the somewhat unhistorical belief, as political reformers, that the next steps were to bring a sharp and sudden improvement, of a kind for which earlier history furnished no parallel. This view, of course, was shared with many reformers of many ages, but for them it became one source of their ambiguity, noted earlier. For if their historical consciousness led to the progressive idea of unending advance, their scientist approach led more naturally to the conservative idea of an optimum about to be reached, at which all would stop, and beyond which no improvement was conceivable. Thus we have elements of progressiveness and elements of conservatism, if not reaction, each representing, in transmuted form, the real interests of a real section of the population. Logically, either could be developed from the Enlightenment. The line of one was represented most powerfully by Voltaire, and some aspects of it were developed by Rousseau, though it received its full eighteenth-century flowering in Burke. The other, optimistic line was represented by the young Turgot and by Condorcet, as well as by Priestley, Paine and Godwin in England.

Voltaire (1694–1778) was the most influential single individual of the Enlightenment, as he was probably also the most successful as a businessman and speculator. Although his main historical works appeared only in the 1750s (the *Siècle de Louis XIV* in 1751, and the *Essai sur les Moeurs et l'Esprit des Nations* in 1756), his earlier writings could with justice be said to have delineated the limits within which the minds of the encyclopedists operated. As a result of his stay in England in 1726–9, he made the doctrines of Locke and Newton the foundation stone on which the theory of the French Enlightenment was based, as he made the 'rational' nature and limited power of the British Government, and the respect in which the merchant class was held, the basis of its political demands.

His history attempted to be universal, and his interest in social and economic developments exposed the errors, follies, and crimes committed by Church and Palace on the people –

History has kept no account of times of peace and tranquillity; it relates only to ravages and disasters ... All history is little else than a long succession of useless cruelties ... a collection of crimes, follies and misfortunes, among which we have now and then met with a few virtues, and some happy times.

By contrast, he wished to know about –

> The tastes and manners of the peoples of the earth and the orderly advance attributable to their organized societies. . .
> The whole wealth of humanity lay in the towns that were scorned by the great rulers. Trade and industry in those towns quietly repaired the damage done by the princes with so much noise.[14]

Thus the progressive principle of history, the source of optimism for the future, lay in the social and economic sphere. He would raise altars to the inventors of the plough, the weaver's shuttle, the carpenter's plane and the saw –

> A lock on a canal joining two seas, a pretence by Poussin, a good tragedy, the discovery of a truth, are a thousand times more precious than all the narratives of campaigns.

Voltaire was not a very systematic thinker, nor, indeed, was he very dogmatic in his views, admitting exceptions and forgiving inconsistencies. Yet in this he remained consistent, that the basis of his history was the constancy of human nature and of human need. If the past showed man's follies, it was his customs and habits which led him to them and his gradual return to reason will liberate him again. The story of customs and habits therefore becomes important, as does the rise of rationality. But the folly and wickedness are social, not individual, and so is the basis of the hope for progress. Voltaire is not certain that man will learn from his experience, nor that reason, and the history that makes sense, will always defeat accidents, chance and the contingent. But the 'laws' of nature point in that direction. As far as rational history and analytical history, or *histoire raisonée* can take us, it points to the likelihood of progress.

Yet in other, and perhaps more significant respects, Voltaire is a conservative. His rigid view of human uniformity, of a

14. *Works* (English edn, 1761), IX, 142, 144; Preface to the *Age of Louis XIV*; J. H. BRUMFITT, *Voltaire: Historian* (1958), p. 69.

unique universal moral law, applicable to all ages, not only led him to 'unhistorical' judgements on the past; it also, in his hands, starkly limits the possibilities of the future. In part, this rigidity is a reflection of the rigidity of Newtonian science: Voltaire's universe, like that of Newton, is static in total and without development. The components are there, and will never change, the world has been set in motion by a single Maker, the machine is working under strict laws, and the most we can do is to understand its working, and use it as intelligently as possible.

But perhaps it also rationalized his own personal preferences. He admired the century of Louis XIV in its glory, and he admired the England of the first two Hanoverians. Perhaps it would not be too much to say that all of previous history was a preparation for the age of the Sun King, when knowledge, medicine, and technology became more rational and education flourished, and music, architecture, painting and sculpture surpassed all previous achievements. Much of the point of his essay on 'Manners' was the contrast between the *misère du passé* and the *bonheur du présent*, which was due to the spread of reason and of moderation. Yet what did this present happiness consist of? It consisted of the comfort and grace, the elegance and culture of the best of French bourgeois existence: a fine house and a good table, paintings and porcelain in the home, the opportunities to converse with other cultured persons or read of the latest discoveries and theories of the philosophers, and some protection from the violence of one's fellow men by the police, and from the violence of disease by doctors. If to this were added political rights and social recognition, and protection from the power of the nobility to have innocent citizens thrown into prison or condemned to exile, the cup of happiness would be full. Voltaire, who had little time for the fashionable admiration of the noble savage, was sure that no civilization with so much to offer had ever existed before; and he found it difficult to imagine that the future could improve on it.

Meinecke, in his perceptive study, finds no difficulty in linking other traits of Voltaire's philosophy with his concept of finality.[15] The very rigidity of his historical judgement, applying to every situation the standards of his own age, is matched by a similar rigidity in the judgement on art or morals. Voltaire's idea of 'perfection', approached in history in only four ages, the Periclean-Alexandrian, Augustan, Medicean and Ludovican, is as unprogressive as it is unscientific. History did not really develop, but merely exhibited the shifting fortunes of the battle between absolute good and absolute evil. And it may be significant that Voltaire thought in terms of human 'talent', consisting of known ingredients, rather than of 'genius', which contains an element of the novel and unpredictable.

Of course, enlightenment had not yet secured a total victory in his time. But it was spreading; the largest part of the journey lay behind them; the Church was being defeated; once it had found its defenders rational enlightenment would become invincible, and this consummation was not far off. At that point we arrive at the conservative, the 'finality' streak in Voltaire's thought. The idea of a fixed system to which all previous development has pointed, and which will not change further once it is reached, is a denial of the idea of progress – though not necessarily of optimism for the future. It represents the local, almost provincial element, as against the universality of historical and social laws. It also represents the fear of the upper bourgeoisie of the demands, the lack of moderation and of 'manners' of the lower orders.

Superficially, the most pessimistic author of the Enlightenment was Rousseau (1712–78), standing in petty bourgeois opposition to the wealthy Voltaire. As he was nurtured in the same soil as the apostles of progress, the factual basis of his philosophy, and his moral views, were much the same as theirs, yet his conclusions appeared to be diametrically opposed. The fur-

15. F. MEINECKE, *Die Enstehung des Historismus* (1946, Munich, 1959 edn), pp. 75 ff. See also JEROME ROSENTHAL, 'Voltaire's Philosophy of History', *J. Hist. Id.* 16 (1955).

ther we progressed towards civilization, it seemed, the further we were from true happiness. The savage

breathes only peace and liberty ... civilized man, on the other hand, is always moving, sweating, toiling, and racking his brains to find still more laborious occupations; he goes on in drudgery to his last moment ... and, proud of his slavery, he speaks with disdain of those, who have not the honour of sharing it.[16]

Rousseau's impassioned plea was for liberty, but his associated demands for democracy and equality were well in advance of the emphasis of the other leading authors, and became among the most powerful ideological influences on the Revolution in France.

But Rousseau, an 'outsider' in his unhappy personal life, tended to exaggerate the gulf between himself and the rest, and has too often been taken at his word in this regard. Others too, like Mably (1709–85), Morellet (1727–1819), and even Diderot were stressing the dangers and evils of luxury, and in 1770, Sebastian Mercier was to project a Utopia for the year 2440 in which happiness was achieved by consuming less (as well as by carrying fewer social parasites and passengers) rather than by producing more.

Further, Rousseau's aim was also ultimately the progress and happiness of mankind, and the development of

human *perfectibility*, the social virtues and the other facilities which natural man potentially possessed.[17]

He merely differed in the methods by which he would achieve them. He distrusted the progress of culture and science, since there was a gulf between the realms of will and of knowledge, between the greed, vanity and lust for power of the world of politics on the one hand, and the harmony of the world of nature on the other. Although he accepted some capitalist values,

16. ROUSSEAU, *Discourse on the Origin of Inequality* (1755), (Everyman edn of *Social Contract and Discourses*, ed. G. D. H. Cole, 1958), p. 220.
17. *Origin of Inequality*, p. 190.

such as the importance of property, he opposed capitalist property relations by the socialist criticism that in them

the interest of every individual dictates rules directly opposite to those the public reason dictates to the community in general – [and] every man finds his profit in the misfortunes of his neighbour.

More generally

the first man who, having enclosed a piece of ground, bethought himself of saying 'This is mine', and found people simple enough to believe him, was the real founder of civil society. From how many crimes, wars and murders, from how many horrors and misfortunes might not anyone have saved mankind, by pulling up the stakes, or filling up the ditch, and crying to his fellows: 'Beware of listening to this impostor; you are undone if you once forget that the fruits of the earth belong to us all, and the earth itself to nobody.'[18]

Rousseau recognized that it was no longer possible to revert to a state of nature, and its praises were merely meant as a critique of present society. Like the encyclopedists, he wanted to preserve and extend what was best in existing civilization, but he saw more pitfalls on the road to progress, and therefore advocated different policies. Among them was an emphasis on equality, stressed in the *Contrat Social* (1762), and on a type of education that would take account of what was best in primitive society, stressed in *Émile*, which appeared in the same year.

Voltaire and Rousseau, in their different ways, represented the pessimistic streak in the French Enlightenment. Before turning to the opposite extreme, the optimism of Turgot and Condorcet, and the idealism which was caught by some German writers, it will be instructive to take the measure of the parallels and differences of thought in Britain. There was, throughout, very close contact and much mutual influence between the two countries, yet British economic and constitutional progress created an environment in which significant differences in thought were bound to emerge.

18. *Origin of Inequality*, pp. 222–3, 192.

In historiography, the moderate scepticism, or Deism, the rationalism, and the emphasis on the contrast between the darkness of the Roman Catholic Middle Ages and the greatness of the civilizations before and after, run without a break from Shaftesbury (1671–1713) and Bolingbroke (1678–1751) to Gibbon (1737–94). As the very title of his main work indicates, Gibbon was interested less in human progress than in the decay of civilizations, or rather, of one particular civilization, destroyed by the 'triumph of barbarism and religion'. Brooding among the ruins of Rome, he felt, like Voltaire who recognized only four ages of human greatness, that the golden moments of humanity are precious and rare, mere islands in a vast ocean of darkness. In the course of his vast survey, he includes many contributing causes of the Decline and Fall, including such economic ones as destructive taxation, but essentially the causes lay not in laws of sociology but in human weakness and vices. Great empires and civilizations, once having risen, must fall again in due course, since human nature remains unchanged over the centuries. The optimism of the French Enlightenment, the preoccupation with the happiness of individuals rather than the grandeur of empires, seems totally missing both in the topic and its treatment.

Yet this would be a misreading both of Gibbon's views and of his contribution. Besides helping to liberate historiography from its narrow and unscientific concentration on the Western world, he made the interplay between West and East, or citizen and 'barbarian', a main theme of his story, thus reintroducing a sociological explanation, and a natural inherent driving force into the process of the rise and fall of civilizations. Moreover, he was as aware of the achievements of his own century as were the French *philosophes*, and inclined to the belief that even if the tide of barbarism washes periodically over the islands of civilization, yet it recedes gradually, leaving more and more of the accumulated achievements of humanity clear of the waves. The gifts of the discoveries of the arts, war, commerce, and religious zeal ... can never be lost. We may therefore acquiesce in the pleasing conclusion, that every age of the World has increased and still increases, the real wealth, the happiness, the knowledge, and perhaps the virtue of the human race.[19]

It was, however, north of the border, in the amazing efflorescence of Scots thought in the eighteenth century, that the French Enlightenment found its closest parallel. Among the debts owed by the *philosophes* to the English-speaking world, the greatest, next to Newton and Locke, was owed to David Hume (1711–76).

Hume based himself on the Lockean sensationalist theory of knowledge, but his mind was too subtle and too sceptical to accept the simple assurances of Newtonian physics. Natural 'laws' are but hitherto observed regularities and sequences in time, which man has set up, since it is easier to believe in laws and regularity than in caprice or in miracles. Since the reliance on observed regularities of the physical world is a social convention – we simply go on assuming that the earth will turn round, and gravity will keep us on the surface of the globe – it is in fact the regularity of behaviour in the social field which gives us the assurance of the reliability of laws of nature.

While there is thus no reason to assume that a Providence has organized our future, and has organized all for the best, there are laws, or regularities, about human behaviour also, and it is the function of the historian, not to relate a story, but to help to discover the laws of the social sciences.

Mankind are so much the same, in all times and places, that history informs us of nothing new or strange in this particular. Its chief use is only to discover the constant and universal principles of human nature by showing men in all varieties of circumstances and situations ... these records of wars, intrigues, factions, and revolutions, are so many collections of experiments, by which the politician or moral philosopher fixes the principles of his science.

19. GIBBON, *Decline and Fall of the Roman Empire* (ed. J. B. Bury, 3rd edn, 1908, 7 vols.), IV, 168–9.

He is helped in this by the regularity of large numbers –

What depends upon few persons is, in a great measure, to be ascribed to chance, as secret and unknown causes; what arises from a great number may often be accounted for by determinate and known causes.[20]

And what are apparently historical accidents and irrational sequences may often merely seem such because of our failure to discover the underlying law.

In view of this brilliant anticipation of much of the best writing on Sociology in the nineteenth century, it is all the more surprising that Hume should have followed the contemporary Enlightenment in dismissing the thousand years of the Middle Ages as a dark period without lessons and without interest for us. Surely social laws can only be confirmed after observing men in 'all varieties of circumstances and situation'?

It has to be admitted that Hume was too much a child of his age to take his own views on the primacy of social laws too seriously. Like Voltaire, he held the implicit belief that all of past history was of value only as a prelude to the greatness of his own times. In the evil past, human behaviour had been irrational, but since the Renaissance opened a winow on the true human world, man's social needs developed the arts, the sciences, and even the morals of society. Only recent European society saw the emergence of freedom, the transformation of the 'government of will' into 'a government of laws'.

Thus history is a battleground, not so much of historical empires or classes, but of tendencies within human psychology, a playground of atomistic forces which sway back and forth, but maintain no single upward direction. In this war of the sword versus the ploughshare, of senseless violence versus rational progress, it was not unreasonable to neglect the lessons of the

20. HUME, 'Enquiry Concerning Human Understanding' in *Enquiries* (ed. L. A. Selby-Bigge, Oxford, 1902 edn), pp. 83–4, and 'Rise and Progress of Arts and Sciences'.

ages of senseless violence. At the same time, we can also see why Hume, who believed that man's other qualities remained constant, that only intellect progressed, and that it alone offered a true insight into human nature and human history, should nevertheless pay so much attention to wealth or the arts, and sciences: they represented the progressive side in his historical dialectic.

Even this, however, leaves a contradiction and it is compounded by others. How is it, for example, that as a Tory he could so much praise the constitution of his own country, all the desirable aspects of which had been procured by the Whig Revolution?

The answer goes deeper than the accident that in Scotland the enemy of progress was not the Tory parson, but the bigoted minister of the 'Whiggamore' Kirk. We cannot understand Hume's position fully unless we think of him as a member of the middle classes which had just achieved some power and status. Hume had to accommodate an intellectual apparatus fashioned for the purpose of helping the bourgeoisie to power – and still being used in France for precisely this purpose – with the social reality of his own country in which the decisive battle was already won, and the road was open to the middle classes. Compare the battles of the French authors with authority with this picture of Britain by a fellow Scot, John Millar –

The memorable Revolution of 1688 ... completed, and reduced into practice, a government of more popular nature, and better fitted to secure the natural rights of mankind, than had ever taken place in a great nation. From this happy period, therefore, commerce and manufacturers assumed a new aspect, and continuing to advance with rapidity, produced innumerable changes in the state of society, and in the character and manners of the people.[21]

21. *Advancement of Manufacturers, Commerce and the Arts*, Appendix to Vol. 4 of *Historical View of the British Government* (4 vols., 1803), reprinted in W. C. LEHMANN, *John Millar of Glasgow* (Cambridge, 1960), p. 326.

While the French stressed the crimes and injustices on which traditional Government, their Government, was based, Hume taught that Governments were created by enlightened self-interest and were therefore utilitarian; it might be right to resist them when they were oppressive rather than beneficial, but he could visualize such an eventuality only *in extremis*. He had to transform a doctrine of assault into a doctrine of defence – perhaps the first who felt acutely the dilemma of the conversion of capitalism from a revolutionary into a conservative force.

In point of fact, only the decisive main battle had been won in Britain, and a vast mopping-up operation had still to be conducted. But the problems of establishing full commercial and industrial freedom by ending the remains of Mercantilism, the protection of the guilds, or the irrational humanitarianism of the Poor Laws, were no longer basic political questions, but questions of economic policy. It was in pursuit of this policy that the British, and especially the Scottish, Enlightenment, developed the science of economics so much more effectively, and with such greater power of generalization than the French, whose economic debate had to be conducted with the main strong-points still in enemy hands. In Hume, we find the first important stirring of this interest in economics, and it is there that his main support for the idea of progress is to be found, while politically he leaned strongly to the conservative, Voltairean wing.

The French believed that, under a system of rational laws, the interests of individuals and of society may be made identical; Hume, like his two Scots compatriots, Adam Smith and Dugald Stewart (1753–1828), takes it that they are. Brushing aside the doubts of Mandeville (1670–1733), Rousseau or Diderot about the possible ill-effects of too much luxury, he believed that an economically advancing society, far from encouraging venality or causing weakness, would promote refinement and truly humane and moral sentiments. Nor is Hume in any doubt what part of the population is the operative agent in this virtuous spiral –

> Where luxury nourishes commerce and industry, the peasants, by a proper cultivation of the land, become rich and independent; while the tradesmen and merchants acquire a share of the property, and draw authority and consideration to that middling rank of men, who are the best and firmest basis of public liberty. These submit not to slavery, like the peasants ... They covet equal laws, which may secure their property, and preserve them from monarchical, as as well as aristocratical tyranny.[22]

On this basis, Hume contributed his share to the gradual liberation of Scottish thinking from the trammels of Mercantilism. His only major original contribution to economics, however, was his insistence on treating every issue from the point of view of society's development, instead of arguing, as did his contemporaries, within a framework of existing static conditions. Here he was not only original: he was far ahead of his time, and it is only now, some two centuries later, that developmental economics has begun to receive similar attention.

By seeing the world evolving on the model of the British economy, Hume was able to throw new light on every single issue. Thus, on the question central to the Mercantilist controversy, the need for large quantities of precious metals in a country, Hume agreed that the absolute quantity did not matter –

> ... the good policy of the Magistrate consists only in keeping it, if possible, still encreasing; because, by that means, he keeps alive a spirit of industry in the nation, and encreases the stock of labour.

It is one of the mainsprings of Hume's optimism that this desirable quality, the 'spirit of industry', grows by what it feeds on –

> Deprive a man of all business and serious occupation, he runs restless from one amusement to another ... But if the employment

22. HUME, 'Of Refinement in the Arts' (1752), in Eugene Rotwein (ed.), *David Hume, Writings on Economics* (1955), pp. 28–9.

you give him be lucrative, especially if the profit be attached to every particular exertion of industry, he has gain so often in his eye, that he acquires, by degrees, a passion for it ... Commerce encreases industry ... It encreases frugality, by giving occupation to men, and employing them in the arts of gain, which soon engage their affection, and remove all relish for pleasure and expence.

In the other Mercantilist issue, that of trade, Hume is a free trader for the same reason, that it will benefit England's growth if her trading partners are prosperous and efficient, rather than backward. Even if their competition reduces the demand for a British manufacture –

... if the spirit of industry be preserved, it may easily be diverted from one branch to another;

moreover, it is by trade that new techniques and inventions spread from one country to another. Similarly, his numerous adverse references to restrictive practices in the *History of England* take the line that their worst effect was the slowing down of progress. Finally, on the question of taxes, Hume noted that where they were moderate and sensibly levied –

... the poor encrease their industry, perform more work, and live as well as before.

Just as it is not always the best endowed nations, but those that are challenged by some difficulties, that are the most progressive ones, and –

therefore some natural necessities or disadvantages may be thought favourable to industry, why may not artificial burdens have the same effect.[23]

The primary consideration is thus the effect on progress, or 'development', to use the current term, into a progressive industrial and commercial economy and the key variable, given

23. The quotations are from Hume's essays 'Of Money' (1752), 'Of Interest' (1752), 'Of the Jealousy of Trade' (1758), and 'Of Taxes' (1752), in Rotwein's edition, pp. 39–40, 55, 59, 80, 83–4.

the general position of the country, is the 'spirit of industry' among the middle and working classes. The treatment of entrepreneurship as the dynamic historic factor was to be greatly extended by Adam Smith, but even in its original form the investigation of the economic stimuli of enterprise, innovation, and hard work for monetary gain, and their effects on progress were far in advance of French thinking which was then still preoccupied with the legal framework permitting capitalist enterprise. We shall return to this issue below; but meanwhile we may note that the great Scottish empiricist came close to denying one of the key principles of eighteenth-century social science (and his own), namely, that human character may be taken as unchanging over the ages. This suggestion was to be obscured again by Adam Smith whose own totally capitalistic environment made him underrate the differences between his and the pre-capitalist societies, and whose 'economic men' are distressingly identical in motivation; but it was to be developed into a cornerstone of the philosophy of the great apostles of unlimited progress, Godwin, Robert Owen and Condorcet.

Adam Ferguson (1723–1816), in the same rationalist, empiricist tradition as Hume, sought to apply the idea of natural law to the social process by which primitive societies had passed through a succession of stages to become the developed civilizations of the eighteenth century. The method of inquiry was to combine the study of surviving primitive societies – an early anthropology – with an attempt to reason back from existing social institutions, on the assumption that social laws and human character remain constant: put an Englishman into a forest, he maintained, and he will behave like an Indian.

Modern social institutions were based partly on social needs – as, indeed, were technical inventions – and they were partly a reflection of inborn human characteristics, human instincts favourable to a social life. But it was important to stress that they were not the result of conscious action, but the conjuncion of numerous individual plans. This key concept, which was attractive to all whose experience was that of a free capitalist market situation, since it described it so well, was to become one of the basic ideas of the new political economy as it related to progress.

Progress for the species as a whole

consists of the continual succession of one generation to another; in progressive attainments made by different ages; communicated with additions from age to age; and in periods, the farthest advanced, not appearing to have arrived at any necessary limit.

Past progress had brought an increase in wealth, in turn dependent on greater division of labour and mutual interdependence, increase in knowledge, and improvement in manners. But since

the *commercial arts* are . . . properly the distinctive pursuit or concern of individuals, and are best conducted on motives of separate interest and private advancement,

it has come about that perhaps the principal characteristic of modern nations entitling them to the epithets 'civilized' and 'polished' was their regard for the individual.[24]

As a philosopher, Ferguson is not sure whether greater wealth will make for a better society, since men may forsake honour for riches and civilized states may be weakened by luxurious living. As an economist, however, he finds it easier to accept that

man is formed with a general disposition to affect what he conceives to be the good . . . He is susceptible of indefinite advancement, engaged in a road of experience and discipline, which points him forward to his end . . . 'progression' . . [is] man's experience from the cradle to the grave.[25]

William Robertson (1721–93), yet another positivist Scots historian and philosopher, started with the proposition that

24 ADAM FERGUSON, *Principles of Moral and Political Science*, 2 vols. (Edinburgh 1782), I, 194, 244 and *Essay on the History of Civil Society* (1773 edn), p. 335.

25. FERGUSON, *Principles*, pp. 141, 183, 184.

human character and sociological laws remained constant. Since therefore peoples in the same conditions will make similar steps towards their perfection and all human beings may potentially be improved, social progress depends on the state of advance reached by society. Robertson insisted even more strongly than Voltaire, that conquerors and tyrants held back human progress, while the useful arts and commerce advanced it and were basically responsible for it, and this was a view shared by much of British historiography in the next century or so.

There were certain obvious dissimilarities between the French and the thinkers of the British Enlightenment. Regarding the role of religion, for example, men could not be unmindful of the fact that the French Church was bitterly hostile to the *philosophes*, while in Britain, Anglicans and Dissenters could tolerantly accept the social views, and even the Deism, of the philosophers. The freedom of the Press could be taken for granted by British subjects, but to the French still had the aura of an inaccessible ideal. There is also the belief of the British (and the Americans) in slow progress, while the French, still standing before their bourgeois revolution, thought in terms of rapid, drastic change. But perhaps the most important, even if the most subtle differences, existed in relation to economic thought. The French could still assume that, once the political and legal framework was changed, benevolent natural laws could ensure that economic progress would take care of itself – where they did not, like the conservative physiocrats, merely posit that the economy would remain much the same, based on agriculture and simple manufactures. In Britain, by contrast, reality had taught that the economy itself was a complex thing that needed careful handling before it could fulfil a progressive role. Further, the positive, progressive role of the bourgeoisie in this period led its philosophers to a depth of understanding of the role of classes, and the mutual interrelations between economic reality and the political superstructure, which was matched again only a hundred years later, in a new context, by Marx.

The most striking accounts of the dynamic relationships involved were given by two other Scotsmen, Lord Kames (1696–1782) and John Millar (1735–1801). In their search for the link between the constant principles of social science and the changing environment of man, they picked on the eternal human driving forces, such as self-love, a desire for action, a desire to improve one's condition of life, as those that will produce material progress. Progress, however, can express itself only in stages of development which are not simply higher editions of earlier ones, but qualitatively different systems, such as the primitive communistic stage, followed by pasturage and the beginnings of property, settled agriculture with slavery or serfdom, and the exchange economy and the specialization of industry, associated with economic freedom. What appears at first sight merely as a stage in economic growth, turns out to be a difference in property and class relations, and each system therefore also corresponds to a different political structure to express its social class relationship. Productive forces determine economic organization, and economic organization in turn determines the class patterns of authority in the State –

The Spirit of liberty appears, in commercial countries, to depend chiefly upon two circumstances: first, the condition of the people relative to the distribution of property, and the means of subsistence: secondly, the facility with which the several members of society are enabled to associate and to act in concert with one another.

The farther a nation advances in opulence and refinement it has occasion to employ a greater number of merchants, of tradesmen and artificers; and as the lower people, in general, become thereby more independent in their circumstances, they begin to exert those sentiments of liberty which are natural to the mind of man, and which necessity alone is able to subdue . . . It cannot be doubted that these circumstances have a tendency to introduce a democratical government. As persons of inferior rank are placed in a situation which, in point of subsistence, renders them little dependent upon their superiors; as no one order of men continues in the exclusive possession of opulence; and as every man who is industrious may entertain the hope of gaining a fortune; it is to be expected that the prerogatives of the monarch and of the ancient nobility will be gradually undermined, that the privileges of the people will be extended in the same proportion, and that power, the usual attendant of wealth, will be in some measure diffused over all the members of the community.[26]

This analysis, describing not only how social laws make change inevitable but also the mechanism which ensures that it is progressive, shows up, by driving to extremes, the basic weakness of all the social science thought of the Enlightenment. This was the assumption that among the unchanging characteristics of human nature, hidden and wrongfully held back in former benighted ages, are all the specific character traits of the bourgeois; that men in other societies, with other value systems and other systems of motivation are in reality, all of them, *bourgeois manqués*.

The belief, enforced by fire and sword, that all men should be made to acknowledge the bourgeois virtues, was to give capitalism its immense proselytizing power in the following two centuries, but meanwhile it drove one stream of the Enlightenment into a cul-de-sac from which it could escape only by a violent change of direction. Up to the arrival of the Scottish political economy, the accusation levelled against the Enlightenment of being unhistorical was in principle unjustified, for the eternal laws and eternal characteristics of human nature the *philosophes* looked for, were in fact those which had remained demonstrably unchanged in historical times. Hume for example saw in the 'spirit of industry' which had to be fostered, and was limited to a certain class only, one of the origins of the

26. JOHN MILLAR, 'The Effects of Commerce and Manufacturers, and of Opulence and Civilizations, upon the Morals of a People'; 'The Advancement of Manufacturers, Commerce, and the Arts, since the Reign of William III' (both appended to Vol. 4 of *A Historical View of the English Government*, 4 vols., first edn, 1803); and *The Origin of the Distinction of Ranks* (1779). The quotations are from the reprints of W. C. LEHMANN, *John Millar*, pp. 383, 330–31, 290, 292.

commercial and economic revolutions that were changing the world and providing the concrete witness of the idea of progress. But according to Adam Smith, the creator of the new thought, all societies, all ages, had the same motivation (even if thwarted) as the successful merchants of his circle. For Adam Smith, and even more so for the economists who followed, every man was by nature a Scotsman on the make.

Perhaps this is unfair to the founder of political economy (though not to his disciples like M'Culloch), for Adam Smith (1723–90) was a pragmatist and rarely committed himself to any statement without noting the exceptions. Moreover, he still had a foot in both camps, for he was reared by his teacher, Francis Hutcheson (1694–1746), to become a part of the brilliant Scottish philosophical Enlightenment, and this is reflected in his *Theory of Moral Sentiments* (1759), which built up human sympathy as the basis of social cohesion. Only in his main work, the *Wealth of Nations* (1776) were social progress, wealth and welfare assured by an individualist struggle in the market place of each against all.

It is possible to bring these two apparent extremes together to some extent. After all, both works were evolved from the same course of lectures and their principles were therefore unlikely to be diametrically opposed. Even in the *Moral Sentiments* we can find such passages as –

Regard to our own private happiness and interest, too, appear upon many occasions very laudable principles of action. The habits of oeconomy, industry, discretion, attention and application of thought, are generally supposed to be cultivated from self-interested motives, and at the same time are apprehended to be very praiseworthy qualities which deserve the esteem and approbation of everybody.[27]

But the contradiction remains and was clearly perceived by John Millar –

27. *Theory of Moral Sentiments* (2 vols., 10th edn, 1804), II, 253–4.

In a rude age, where there is little industry, or desire of accumulation, neighbouring independent societies are apt to rob and plunder each other; but the members of the same society are attracted by a common interest, and are often strongly united in the bands of friendship and affection, by mutual exertions of benevolence, or by accidental habits of sympathy. But in a country where nobody is idle, and where every person is eager to augment his fortune, or to improve his circumstances, there occur innumerable competitions and rivalships, which contract the heart, and set mankind at variance. In proportion as every man is attentive to his own advancement, he is vexed and tormented by every obstacle to his prosperity, and prompted to regard his competitors with envy, resentment, and other malignant passions . . .

That there is no friendship in trade is an established maxim among traders. Every man for himself, and God Almighty for us all, is their fundamental doctrine.[28]

However, his own experience made it easy for Adam Smith to accept that wealth and morals went hand in hand. The struggle of the market place, so hateful and destructive in Rousseau's eyes, had produced the comfort, the civilization, the unexampled efflorescence of Scotland which the Scots professor saw around him. Thus wealth promoted morals, and as Scottish experience showed, the replacement of a traditional society by a competitive one promoted greater wealth. Private and social interest coincided, competition promoted the good, moral society, and with the help of a technical discussion in the light of which the French *savants* appear as naïve amateurs, Adam Smith had no difficulty in convincing himself that

every individual . . . neither intends to promote the public interest, nor knows how much he is promoting it . . . by directing . . . industry in such a manner as its produce may be of the greatest value, he intends only his own gain, and he is in this, as in many other cases, led by an invisible hand to promote an end which has no part of his intention.

Indeed, he continues,

nor is it always the worse for the society that it was no part of it. By pursuing his own interest he frequently promotes that of the society more effectually than when he really intends to promote it. I have never known much good done by those who affected to trade for the public good. It is an affectation, indeed, not very common among merchants, and very few words need be employed in dissuading them from it.

Moreover, even the most selfish accumulation of riches could not increase inequality, for the capacity of the human stomach is limited, and as a man becomes richer, he spends his wealth in keeping more servants or employees at a reasonable standard of living. For

the rich only select from the heap what is most precious and agreeable . . . They are led by an invisible hand to make nearly the same distribution of the necessities of life which would have been made had the earth been divided into equal proportions among all its inhabitants, and thus, without intending it, without knowing it, advance the interests of society, and afford means to the multiplication of the species . . . In what constitutes the real happiness of human life, [the poor] are in no respect inferior to those who would seem so much above them.[29]

The extreme partisanship for *laissez-faire* evident in these passages was, contrary to public belief, never part of the fixed canon of the science founded by Adam Smith. Smith's compatriot, Sir James Steuart (1712–80) brought up in the same climate of opinion, whose major work, the *Principles of Political Oeconomy*, appeared nine years before the *Wealth of Nations*, advocated a moderate Mercantilism with great skill, and Smith himself admitted important exceptions to his own rules. Elsewhere, whenever countries in certain stages of development or groups of entrepreneurs could profit from protection or

29. *Wealth of Nations* (Cannan, ed, 2 vols., 6th edn, 1961), I, 477; *Moral Sentiments*, II, 385–6.

State initiative, there have been political economists who have defended these policies. By contrast, the belief that capitalism is a better system than that which it replaced, has always been firmly part of the canon. The great Scotsman gazed upon far-away countries, and contemplated the history of past centuries of his own, and he concluded, like Voltaire and like Gibbon, that his own age and country were superior to anything else the world had yet seen. The transformation which made, or would make them, like his own, was progress, and he set out to describe how it was achieved, and how it could be continued. In other words, he was largely concerned with what we today would call economic development.

In the earliest known form taken by his thoughts, in his lectures delivered no later than 1759, he discussed the causes of the slow progress of opulence, in spite of the benefits derived from the division of labour. He enumerated 'material impediments', that is the lack of capital and the 'oppression of civil government', under which heading he grouped wars and anarchy, slavery and serfdom, short tenancies, high taxes and obstruction of trade, privileges and monopolies, legal insecurity, the low social esteem of merchants and poor transport facilities. When he developed the same thoughts in the *Inquiry into the Nature and Causes of the Wealth of Nations* in 1776, there was no major change in his views. Mercantilist restrictionism and aristocratic abuses were still the main enemies. The world of 1776 is still essentially that of an agrarian country, in which manufactures are carried on by independent craftsmen or putting-out merchants and not yet in factories. Capital is still desperately scarce, and since it is indispensable in extending the division of labour, which in turn is the main engine of economic progress, it has to be husbanded with the greatest care. Thus capitalists, who save, are benefactors of society, and landowners, who tend to consume, are not; and the expansion of agriculture, in which little capital will create much employment, is much preferable to investment in industry, where it will employ less labour, and still more so, to investment in trade and shipping where it will employ least.

If Adam Smith is at his best in his historical chapters, he is at his weakest in attempting to discern the shape of things to come. He promises himself certain benefits from the abolition of all restrictions and privileges, from the return of capital away from trade, and back to its 'natural employment' in agriculture, and from certain specific improvements in education and training; but apart from this, the future offers little that is new. Above all, the political and social structure of Britain and the property relationships were accepted as fixed. It was precisely because of this fixed framework that Adam Smith could begin to manipulate the economic variables – land, labour, capital – in the new, scientific and generalized way which marked the decisive advance over the French Physiocrats.

The historical and descriptive chapters are concerned with development and economic progress. Book I is entitled: 'Of the Causes of the Improvement in the productive powers of labour, and of the order of the People', and Book III, an enlargement of the section of the lectures mentioned above, is entitled, 'Of the different Progress of Opulence in Different Nations'. Book I, Chapter XI, on Rent, discusses the effects of 'the progress of wealth and improvement' on the prices of different kinds of agricultural produce and manufactured goods. More significant still, the whole concept of rent can be understood only in an evolutionary context, in the change from society 'in its rude beginnings', to a modern economy. Again, agricultural progress may be linked with the progress from slavery, via *métavage* and insecure tenancies, to secure tenancies. The rise of the town as a political and economic unit after the fall of the Roman Empire, is treated historically followed by an account 'How the Commerce of the Town Contributed to the Improvement of the Country' (Book III, Chapter IV).[30] Among the reasons for this

30. ADAM SMITH, *Lectures on Justice, Police, Revenue and Arms* (ed. Cannan, Oxford, 1896), pp. 222–36.

last are that towns provided markets; that merchants buy land, and as they are 'accustomed to employ [their] money chiefly in profitable projects ... they are generally the best of all improvers'; and finally –

Commerce and manufactures gradually introduced order and good government, and with them, the liberty and security of individuals, among the inhabitants of the country, who had before lived almost in a continual state of war with their neighbours, and of servile dependency upon their superiors.

After tracing changes in the incomes, expenditure, legal powers and social powers of these two classes, Smith continues –

A revolution of the greatest importance to the public happiness, was in this manner brought about by two different orders of people, who had not the least intention to serve the public. To gratify the most childish vanity was the sole motive of the great proprietors. The merchants and artificers much less ridiculous, acted merely from a view to their own interest and in pursuit of their own pedlar principle of turning a penny wherever a penny was to be got ... It is thus that through the greater part of Europe the commerce and manufacture of cities, instead of being the effect, have been the cause and occasion of the improvement and cultivation of the country.[31]

After this sociological analysis of the role of the capitalist entrepreneur, Book V, the final one, treats of the part played by the political authority in economic welfare and progress, and of taxation. They, again, assume the bourgeois social framework of his own time.

We are therefore faced with the same ambiguity we noted in the French Enlightenment, between an immanent, analytically necessary upward movement in the past, and the assumption of a fixed future: once again progress depends on the tense. However, there is now a significant difference, for while total social

31. *Wealth of Nations*, I, pp. 432–3, 440. The reference to 'happiness' is significant here, as in general Smith deals with 'wealth', and on his own terms they are by no means synonymous. Again, 'merchants and artificers' is a significant description of the bourgeoisie.

changes stop in the present, purely economic changes continue. The capitalist system, with its appropriate legal and political framework, is the end of social evolution; but economic progress within it may go on. This progress will be quantitative rather than qualitative. Rents, profits and wages will continue to be the categories of income, but their levels may rise. This may not be progress in the sense in which the encyclopedists had envisaged it, but it is progress still.

With Adam Smith we reach the parting of the ways. Henceforth, the unity of social philosophy is broken. British political economy (in due course to become 'economics') has taken off on a course of its own, manipulating with growing skill increasingly mobile variables within an increasingly rigid social framework. The system of value judgements, of personal and class relations, the power structure, the property relations, the attitude to science and technology – all these, and many more, making up capitalism as a 'type' of society of internally consistent character in the Weberian sense, were taken for granted by the new economic science. In the England of Ricardo, let alone of Nassau Senior or of Jevons and Marshall, they could indeed be taken for granted, but the link with history has disappeared.

The increasing neglect of history by economists did not mean that they turned their backs on the idea of progress. On the contrary, having incorporated it within their mental framework, they spent their time on methods of achieving it. This was true at least as long as capitalism remained an obviously progressive system, offering even greater material benefits to society; it was necessarily less true in periods of depression and recession, as for examples in the 1920s and 1930s. But meanwhile the contact between the two thought worlds of the historians and the economists had been broken.

It is time now to retrace our steps and resume the main line of argument. We have seen how it was possible to base, on the corpus ideas of the Enlightenment, philosophies of stagnation, mirrored to some extent in British political economy, both being anchored to the interests of fundamentally satisfied classes. We must now turn to the other extreme, to the most optimistic line of philosophers, who expected progress not only in knowledge, in wealth or in social organization alone, but even improvement in the character and nature of human beings themselves.

In England, optimism could be the outcome both of agnostic and of religious thought. William Paley (1743–1805) was certain of growing social happiness because that is what God intended. The mechanism by which it would be brought about was the association of ideas, derived from Hartley, which could transform the base metal of egotism into benevolence, and the framework was the British Constitution as fixed by the revolution of 1689. Other religious perfectionists were Bishop Butler (1692–1752) and Richard Price (1723–91).

As the high point of optimism in the 1790s approached, however, the Churches began to line up against a new philosophy which at that stage looked as though it might threaten the social fabric, and the mantle fell on agnostics and Unitarians. Priestley (1733–1804), a minister of religion who had his house sacked by a Church and King mob in 1791, and became one of the most distinguished British refugees from political repression, derived his extreme optimism like Paley, from the conviction that God intended human happiness –

We ought to take for granted, the doctrines of the wisdom and goodness of God, as suggested from his works and his word. Let an historian, therefore, attend to every instance of improvement, and a better state of things brought about . . . in history, and let him ascribe those events to an *intention* in the Divine Being to bring about that better state of things by means of those events; and if he cannot see the same benevolent tendency in all other appearances let him remain in suspense with regard to them.[32]

After all, even wars might be beneficial by bringing barbarians into contact with civilization, and end their sloth and indolence,

32. JOSEPH PRIESTLEY, *Lectures on History and General Policy* (Birmingham, 1783), pp. 530–51.

and the history of the Borgias, sometimes cited to confound the optimist, showed the full power of Divine Providence: for were not both father and son poisoned in error, by the wine prepared for their enemies? Priestley could find some good even in the bleakness of the Middle Ages: the Popes preserved some learning, the monks helped to found towns, and the crusades helped to curb the powers of the Barons.

In the course of the recent centuries, since the production of gunpowder, the discovery of America, and the circumnavigations, Europe had witnessed great advances in the arts and commerce and in wealth. There were greater comforts, better food, dress and habitation, more refined manners and, in consequence, more happiness. 'A *numerous*, a *secure*, and a *happy* society is the object of all human policy', and we were superior to the ancients in having more liberty and security. Bad Government is the result of ignorance and prejudice; with knowledge and reason, 'the minds of men are opening to large and generous views of things', and Governments can become the 'great instrument of progress' – largely by leaving things alone. In Britain, an ideal constitution was created by the revolution under King William.[33] It was his known belief that the French were experiencing a similar millennial revolution that caused his unpopularity and persecution.

If wealth was to create good Government, and good Government to promote the creation of more wealth, the outside agency that would keep the movement going in an upwards spiral was science –

of which the human faculties cannot conceive the possibility of any bounds.

The rapid progress of knowledge which ... extends itself ... *in all directions*, will, I doubt not, be the means under God, of extirpating all error and prejudice ... in the business of *religion* as well as of Science ... There certainly never was any period in which

33. ibid., pp. 271, 263, 11–12.

natural knowledge made such a progress as it has done of late years, and especially in this country.

Knowledge as Lord Bacon observes, being power, the human powers will, in fact, be enlarged; nature, including both its materials and its laws, will be more at our command; men will make their situation in this world abundantly more easy and comfortable; they will probably prolong their existence in it, and will grow daily more happy, each in himself, and more able (and I believe, more disposed) to communicate happiness to others. Thus whatever was the beginning of this world, the end will be glorious and paradisiacal beyond what our imaginations can now conceive.[34]

Most of the other English optimists of the period, including Priestley's friend, Erasmus Darwin (1731–1802), and William Godwin (1756–1836), were freethinkers. Godwin has been called a Utopian rather than a believer in progress, but his state of perfection was a long way off, and required a slow process of evolution and amelioration. It was Godwin who translated the French idea of 'perfectibility' most correctly in terms of evolution rather than Utopia –

... man is perfectible, or, in other words, susceptible of perpetual improvement.

Once establish the perfectibility of man, and it will inevitably follow that we are advancing to a state, in which truth will be too well known to be easily mistaken, and justice too habitually practised to be voluntarily counteracted.

Man, in fact, was 'perfectible' in that sense, since he was a creature of the circumstances of his upbringing and environment

nothing can be more unreasonable than to argue from men as we now find them to men as they may hereafter be made.[35]

34. *Lectures on History*, p. 382; *Experiments and Observations on Different Kinds of Air* (1775), 3 vols., I, xiv-xv; *Essay on the First Principles of Government* (1768), pp. 4–5 reprinted in IRA V. BROWN, *Joseph Priestley, Selections from his Writings* (Pennsylvania, 1962), pp. 152–3.

35. GODWIN, *Enquiry Concerning Political Justice* (1793), (1796 edn, 2 vols.), I, 87, II, 116–17.

With this defiant belief that not only knowledge, science, wealth, social organization and moral behaviour, but man himself is indefinitely improvable, we reach the highest point of the idea of progress, for we surely cannot go beyond the progress of the species itself. It required an unshakeable optimism, and it is significant that Godwin, like Condorcet, the other philosopher who most clearly held to it, was not dismayed by the convulsions of the French Revolution. When many others faltered in their optimism, Godwin stood fast, and saw no reason to change the views of the first edition of *Political Justice* of 1793 for the editions 1796 and 1798.

Godwin's confidence derived from his belief in the power of the intellect, while the human mind was as subject to law, to necessity and predictability, as was physical matter. Given this extreme determinism, it follows that our present imperfections stem from the inadequate dominance of reason. Since reason not only sees what is right, but irresistibly urges action towards that end, we shall, with the growth of science and knowledge, approach ever more closely to perfection. Thus the more we know, the more moral we shall be, and the more nearly shall we be able to work out with mathematical certainty the preconditions for our happiness –

Nothing further is requisite but the improvement of [man's] reasoning faculty, to make him virtuous and happy.

Striking support for this thesis was to derive almost at once from the most famous attack on Godwin, Malthus's *Essay on Population*. This had set out to destroy Godwin's dream of happiness by warning that as soon as material conditions were easier, population would increase until it outgrew the food supply, and thus plunged back into poverty and misery. Godwin used his own principles to retort that a wiser population would voluntarily and painlessly restrain its increase, and he had the satisfaction of seeing that Malthus was constrained to adopt much the same view in the second edition of his essay.

Yet Godwin admitted one danger. Social evils and ignorance had been rampant in the past, and the inevitable process of advance will, it is true, lead to truth and goodness, but Governments, by their nature, look backwards, as if it were the nature of the human mind always to degenerate and never to advance. Hence all government is harmful to human character. A people which is beginning to learn morality, the science of human happiness and the nature of social interdependence, has no need of the evil of Government –

everything may be trusted to the tranquil and wholesome progress of knowledge, and . . . the office of the enlightened friend of political justice, for the most part, consists in this, a vigilant and perpetual endeavour to assist the progress.[36]

Godwin, however, lacked any consistent thought as to how to effect the transition except for the petty-bourgeois equation of liberty with anarchy and the universal panacea of education. The book, though priced at no less than three guineas, sold four thousand copies, a proof of the eagerness with which it was read by sections of the middle classes. Nevertheless, because of the political repression which followed, its immediate impact in Britain was slight apart from the influence upon the Lake Poets, with whom its sentiments began to enter upon their inevitable transformation into romanticism.

It is doubtful whether Godwin had much influence on Robert Owen, (1771–1858), particularly since the latter claimed to have evolved all his philosophy himself, but the likeness between them is unmistakable. In many respects still an eighteenth-century mind, Owen opened a new era of thought by including the factory proletariat among the 'people' about whom history is written and political decisions are made, and this squarely put him into the nineteenth century.

Owen's central doctrine that 'man's character was made *for* him, not *by* him', led him to give overriding power to early

36. *Political Justice*, I, pp. 245, 382, 306–7, 361–2.

education and upbringing. To illustrate the point, he used the example of the judges and the criminals. If the present judges had been brought up 'among the poor and profligate of St Giles' they would certainly, 'have already suffered imprisonment, transportation, or death'; and

if some of those men whom the laws dispensed by the present judges have doomed to suffer capital punishment, had been born, trained, and circumstanced as these judges were born, trained and circumstanced, ... [they] would have been the identical individuals who would have passed the same awful sentences on the present highly esteemed dignitaries of the law.

More important still, this law was true not only for individuals, but also for society –

Any general character, from the best to the worst, from the most ignorant to the most enlightened, may be given to any community, even to the world at large, by the application of proper means; which means are to a great extent at the command and under the control of those who have influence in the affairs of men.[37]

It was, therefore, not the slow and inevitable growth of science or knowledge which would create the good society, but the total, and perhaps artificially created, correct environment. This view could have come to grief at once over the problem of action, since human benevolence could not arise in the existing immoral environment, and yet, without it, the environment could not be changed; but Owen held implicitly to the Enlightenment doctrine that even in the present immoral world, men have only to be shown the way to moral conduct in order to adopt it, so that change would come dramatically by the mere announcement of his correct doctrine.

Owen's original appeal was to his fellow manufacturers and other men of power and influence. It was largely by a series of events outside his control that he found himself the spokesman,

37. ROBERT OWEN, 'Essays on the Formation of Character', in *A New View of Society and Other Writings* (Everyman edn, 1927), pp. 16, 25.

not of the shopkeepers and merchants and farmers or peasants, whose battle cry was 'liberty', but of the class below them in society, whose battle cry was still more elementary: 'bread'. It was for these that he made the transition from bourgeois to proletarian idealism, from the eighteenth to the nineteenth century.

In France, the ultimate in optimism was reached by Condorcet, but many of his ideas were anticipated in a brilliant *tour de force* of Turgot (1727–81), written when he was still a student. Turgot, though personally drawn to study and research, had some opportunity of turning the ideas of the Enlightenment into reality by becoming one of France's most brilliant administrators. When he became supreme economic Minister to Louis XVI, his progressive bourgeois policies for the two years, from 1774–6, kindled the greatest hopes among the *savants*: 'Nous touchons au temps où les hommes vont commencer a devenir raisonnables', wrote Voltaire.[38] The privileged nobles and prelates, however, counter-attacked savagely, and drove him from office. But his work had directed his later interests largely to economic questions in which, indeed, he exerted a great influence on Adam Smith. His views on history have to be judged mainly from his youthful essays, the lecture on the 'Advances of the Human Mind', and the notes on 'Universal History' (both of 1750).

The lecture, or discourse, packs with remarkable economy of words a complete philosophy of progress into a very small compass. His world is one of science, rationalism and constant human qualities, and progress will derive from improved social organization which will get the most out of existing material –

The science of government will then become easy, and will cease to be beyond the reach of men endowed with only ordinary good sense.[39]

The growth will not be in individual powers, but in social

38. BRUMFITT, *Voltaire*, p. 126.
39. TURGOT, *Pensées*, reprinted in W. W. Stephens' *The Life and Writings of Turgot* (1895), p. 317.

wisdom, inevitable since each generation learns from all past experience. Empires and civilizations rise and decline but something positive always remains. Barbarians, even when they appear as conquerors, learn from the civilizations they vanquish –

in the midst of their savages manners are gradually softened, the human mind takes enlightenment ... and the total mass of the human race ... marches always, although slowly, towards still higher perfection.

The stream, it is true, sometimes disappears underground. From the heights of Rome, Europe declined to the crude barbarism of the Middle Ages, but the Arabs preserved the Greek heritage, and out of that decline came the rise towards the present civilizations. It began with the development of agriculture, leading to permanent settlements and ultimately towns, which in turn permitted the rise of commerce and the accompanying division of labour. Among the new specializations is science, invention itself, as 'grotesque speculations' end with the Renaissance and the arts and practical experience combine to further new rational knowledge. In the last few hundred years mankind advanced far beyond the classical period, the important inventions including the

... art of recording music, our bills of exchange, our paper, window glass, plate glass, windmill, clocks, spectacles, gunpowder and the magnetic needle leading to the perfection of navigation and commerce.

The process, once begun, will inevitably move forward in the future also –

... the evils inseparable from revolutions disappear, the good remains, and Humanity perfects itself.[40]

The analysis is tighter, fits together better than that of Turgot's predecessors, and has a much more modern ring. In addi-

40. TURGOT, *On the Successive Advances of the Human Mind* (1750), in Stephens, op. cit., pp. 160, 170, 162.

tion, however, Turgot also deals fruitfully with two of the logical problems concerned with his analysis. One concerns the sociology of invention. How can progress be predicted, when it depends on invention which is chancy and therefore unpredictable? The answer is the social law that among mechanics, there are always some 'of genius who are mixed with the rest of mankind', and who are fertile when conditions are ripe. When they are not, genius remains undiscovered and it appears that their society lacked talent: if Corneille had been brought up a plough-boy, or Racine among the Canadian Huron, their powers would never have been called into being. Thus innovation depends on the general state of society.

The other, and more basic problem, was the relation between the scientific and the historical, the generalized and the unique. History, states Turgot, should

embrace the consideration of the successive progressions of the human race and of the detail of the causes that have contributed to them

since the beginning of man. At the same time, however, we wish it

to unveil the influence of general and necessary causes, along with that of particular causes, and that of the free action of great men, to discover the springs and mechanism of moral causes by their effects.[41]

The bridge between these two approaches to history is to realize that while the natural talents of humanity are everywhere the same, and operate within the framework of fixed social laws, the circumstances and, above all, the preceding history differ, so that the particular characteristics of each society are the inevitable consequences of its own immediate past. Thus the particular and the general collaborate in providing a mechanism for human progress.

41. *Notes on Universal History* in STEPHENS, op. cit., p. 175; *Advances of the Human Mind*, p. 161.

This philosophical dualism, or interplay between the fixed and the contingent, is applicable equally to the human mind itself –

Ni mos idées ni nos sentiments ne sont innés : mais ils sont *naturels*, fondés sur la constitution de notre esprit et de notre âme et sur nos rapports avec tout ce qui nous environne.[42]

Turgot has often been termed a positivist and, with Condorcet, a direct forerunner of Comte. The very title of Turgot's essay refers to the advances of the mind, rather than of humanity, and it was great minds that altered history –

the light that a man of letters can shed must, sooner or later, destroy all the artificial evils of mankind, and enable men to enjoy all the goods offered them by nature.[43]

For a similar reason, he held education to be fundamental among his proposed reforms. In the first stages of development of the human mind, men thought that the world around them was moved by superhuman beings, invisible and more powerful than they (Comte's 'theological' stage). At a second, higher stage, philosophers saw the absurdity of fables about the gods, and instead used abstractions, such as 'essences' and 'faculties' (Comte's 'metaphysical' stage). But finally, men emerged to observe the real world, and formulated scientific laws, with action verified by experience and mathematics (Comte's 'positive' stage). In this last stage, particularly because of the existence of specialist scientists, the printed page, and organizations such as Academies, progress based on new technology would vastly accelerate.

Turgot personifies the French bourgeoisie in the full flower of its hope. Things were getting better, the Government was attempting various reforms, and Turgot saw the State apparatus, not like many other *philosophes* from the inside of a prison cell, but from high administrative office. If men need only to be

42. Letter to Condorcet, December 1773. CHARLES HENRY (ed.), *Correspondance inédite de Condorcet et Turgot, 1770–1779* (Paris, 1883).
43. Letter to Condorcet, 21 June 1772. HENRY, op. cit., pp. 88–9; translated in STEPHENS, op. cit., pp. 275–6.

shown the good and just action to perform it, then it would not be long before the ideals of the bourgeoisie, which to him seemed self-evidently superior, would be put into practice. The reforms would bring about, not merely greater wealth, but also that most elusive of aims, greater happiness. To quote his *Pensées* again –

the interests of nations and the success of good government reduce themselves to a sacred respect for the liberty of persons and of labour, to the inviolable maintenance of the rights of property, to justice between all, from which condition necessarily result a greater production of things useful to man, the increase of wealth, and of enjoyments, and of enlightenment and all the means of happiness.[44]

The assurance that the bourgeois political and economic demands constituted the ultimate in justice and human rights did not, any more in France than in England, outlast the eighteenth century. It was to find its apogee in the work of Condorcet (1743–94). His *Sketch for a Historical Picture of the Progress of the Human Mind* (1795) makes its impact not only by the absolute confidence in humanity and its irresistible progress, but also by the striking, almost romantic conditions under which it was written. It had been dashed off in one searing spell of hope and defiance, while he was in hiding for some nine months, without outside contacts and without access to books, in the interval between his public disgrace after being President of the Legislative Assembly, and his miserable death in a police cell. The contrast between the squalor of his actual existence, and the fervent and noble optimism of his thoughts, could not but strike the imagination of his readers.

Despite his passion and his idealism, Condorcet believed his view of history to be firmly anchored in rationalism, and in science. The world was governed by discoverable natural laws, and one of these was the inevitability of progress. This could be established both inductively and deductively, and one of Con-

44. Reprinted in STEPHENS, op. cit., p. 316.

dorcet's most striking contributions is his account of past history in terms of analytical progress. His ten stages and their causal sequences form a dynamic mixture of materialist and idealist ingredients, but on the whole it is the ideas which are dominant in determining human progress. They represent an interim stage in the development of Positivism from Turgot to Comte, and may be summarized as the evolutionary sequence of four human explanations of the world, the anthropomorphic and theological, the metaphysical, the mechanistic-materialistic, and the mathematical-scientific. Each of the four mental attitudes corresponds to a certain degree of happiness, for just as the last one accelerates the production of material comforts and improvements, so the earlier ones furthered ignorance and vice.

Of his ten historical stages, the first was the primitive tribal stage. It developed into the second, or pastoral stage, which was inevitably turning to agriculture, with its necessary accompaniment of a class system, leading to deceit and robbery. The third stage, possessing developed agricultural settlement, made its population vulnerable to domination by conquerors, but also saw the invention of the alphabet. The fourth stage was that of Greece, culminating in the division of the sciences, but the Greeks, instead of creating the precise terms which science required, used everyday words and therefore landed in casuistry instead of scientific precision. In the fifth stage, the rise of Christianity brought about the decline of science. The sixth stage saw science in decay until the Crusades, though the Arabs transmitted and developed Greek culture, especially in chemistry, pharmacy and algebra. However, one positive contribution of Europe was the ending of slavery.

In the seventh stage occurred the slow revival of science leading to the invention of printing, though religion was still powerful enough to stultify reason. The eighth stage saw the fall of Constantinople and the discovery of the New World, but more decisively, it also witnessed how printing aided the victory of the new science in the realm of natural phenomena, though not yet in issues affecting politics and religion. The ninth stage ran from Descartes to the foundation of the French Republic, and the tenth was that of the future, to which the *Sketch* as a whole was, in a sense, devoted.

The division and emphasis of these different states, it will be observed, has no logical unity, and categories of a very different nature are thrown together. The earlier ones, for example, depend on systems of production, and the later on scientific progress. But it was Condorcet's merit that in his vision of history as a sequence of types of society, each arises logically and necessarily from the preceding one, and each inevitably carries within itself the seeds of the next one to come. The sequence as a whole, moreover, obeys a logical order and the past stages can therefore be used to forecast the future ones.

This amounted to a new type of history –

Up to now, the history of politics ... has been the history of only a few individuals: that which really constitutes the human race, the vast mass of families living for the most part on the fruits of their labour, has been forgotten ... In writing the history of individuals, it is enough to collect facts; but the history of a group of men must be supported by observations; and to select these observations and to fasten upon their essential features enlightenment is necessary and ... philosophy in the same measure.[45]

Progress, though based on knowledge and science, was not for Condorcet a purely intellectual or technological matter. On the contrary, it was progress above all in morals and in happiness precisely because knowledge aids the growth of virtue, while vice is the result of ignorance which, when it is once dispersed, cannot return. Human sympathy, in fact, is 'natural', constant over the ages and universal, arising from the needs of the child, and it spreads with adulthood to the whole of society, not because of a revelation, but because of the growth of human faculties.

In a way, what has to be explained is the deplorable story of

45. CONDORCET, *Sketch* (1955 edn), p. 170.

man's past, rather than the certainty of a better future. Condorcet believes that it was largely due to the hereditary transmission of power and to religion, which permitted priests to use their hold over men's minds to preserve reactionary governments. Corrupt governments made their people corrupt, and thus civilizations might slip back, or be swallowed up by larger, though less advanced neighbours. On the intellectual plane, primitive societies had no specialist class of thinker, nor could hunters and fishers take off time for developing their own minds, so that over long ages the development of the human mind, and therefore of human social organization, was retarded. Also –

according to the general laws of development of our faculties, certain prejudices have necessarily come into being at each stage of our progress.[46]

In the early stages primitive and anthropomorphic views of the physical environment held up the growth of knowledge; later, it was retarded by cultural lag or by the survival of classes or specialists who once filled a progressive role, but were overtaken by developments, yet preserved some obstructive power, and he named the priesthood as an example.

But recently, the foundations of more rapid progress have been laid by the development of agriculture, private property, exchange, industry, the division of labour, making possible the rise of scientists and philosophers, the growth of population, the invention of writing. Before long, discoveries will be further speeded up by the creation of a new scientific language. As the advances in science accelerate, useful inventions will increasingly be made systematically and not, as in the past, by accident. More significantly, the benefits will spread to the social and moral sciences, partly by a direct fall-out of techniques, such as the use of the calculus of probability in politics or decision-making, and mainly because of the wholly new mental and moral attitudes engendered.

46. *Sketch*, p. 11.

The new philosophers will be aware of the rights of man, which derive from the single truth that man is a sentient being, capable of reasoning, of acquiring moral ideas, but also of finite understanding, based on his experience. They will free men's mind from superstition, and the political and moral errors based on it. They will greatly enrich the capacity of the next generation of children by more rational education, and end the harmful belief that all was known that could be known, for 'nature has set no limits to the realization of our hopes'. Everywhere around him, Condorcet could see colonialism and slavery breaking down, inequality between nations and within nations being lessened. As better generalizations and new statements of scientific laws were being developed, they would spread the knowledge of science more easily and more widely, better technologies were raising economic output and welfare, and when the benefits spread to the social arts and sciences, there would come a lessening of prejudices, of harmful customs and of national aggression. Ultimately the effects of progress in all fields will react on each other –

As preventive medicine improves, and food and housing becomes healthier, as a way of life is established that develops our physical powers by exercise without ruining them by excess, as the two most virulent causes of deterioration, misery and excessive wealth, are eliminated, the average length of human life will be increased and a better health and stronger physical constitution will be ensured.[47]

Life expectancy will rise, and even man's mental powers will be improved, in part by education, and in part, perhaps, genetically.

What then does Condorcet, the last heir of the optimism of the French Enlightenment, mean by 'progress'? In the scientific-methodological sense he may be said to have envisaged three separate, though linked, advances: the simple linear accumulation of ideas with more experience; a struggle in which reason defeats its enemies one by one; and the power of the scientific

47. *Sketch*, p. 199.

method as such, at any time, to deal with the corpus of inherited ideas. But this is merely the intellectual sub-stratum of his faith. In more human terms, he envisaged an increase in happiness or a reduction of pain. This was not merely a crude Utilitarian principle, for it linked very closely social with individual well-being, it associated art, knowledge, and spiritual greatness with physical satisfaction and bodily health, and it made the process of becoming, of achieving and moving towards a better society, the operative element in 'happiness'.

It is a measure of Condorcet's genius that, in all essentials, liberal-democratic Western Society still preserves long-term purposes laid down by him, and that his short-term demands have in fact been fulfilled in a remarkably large number of areas. Western society now accepts universal education, universal suffrage, equality before the law, freedom of thought and expression, freedom and self-determination for colonial peoples, national insurance and pensions, and equal rights for women; and a large section of it also holds greater equality of incomes to be desirable. If the nineteenth century, in the fullness of its own historicism, criticized Condorcet for basing himself on a 'natural', inevitable trend towards progress yet impatiently urging and applauding a violent revolution, it merely showed its inability to understand the social pressures building up under the kind of stranglehold represented by the *ancien régime*. This dilemma was to face all prophets of progress in an oppressively reactionary state, until theory and practice were brought together in the Marxian dialectic, in which revolution becomes the 'natural' form of change.

Thus the thought of the Enlightenment entered the nineteenth century in two main guises: British political economy, and French revolutionary Radicalism. There was also a third stream, less powerful, perhaps, in historical terms, but not without influence: German idealist philosophy. That the German lines of thinking should differ from the French and the British was not surprising, for while the British had achieved their bourgeois society and the French were within sight of it, the spokes-men of the German bourgeoisie were not only without such a base, but could scarcely visualize a modern unified, let alone a democratic, German State. It was easier to transfer their hopes to ideals, to concentrate on a conversion of the spirit rather than on the outward trimmings of new constitutions in dozens of separate capitals, and to be more impressed by solutions to theoretical problems than by concrete economic issues which scarcely existed in more than embryonic form.

The ideas of Kant (1724–1804) are most recognizably in the French liberal tradition. In a brilliantly compressed essay, *The Idea of a Universal History on a Cosmopolitan Plan* (1784), he accepted human progress as a

steady and continuous, though slow, development of certain great dispositions in our nature.

The progress of man was laid down by the 'will of nature', and the fate which nature has in store for man, was for him to use his reason in order to build up his own future. The driving force is the system of tensions within society and man's ambivalence in being both sociable and antisocial. As any society will throw up a leader and tyrant, historical evolution consists of devising a constitution, or system of laws, to restrain him and develop the ideal civil society founded on political justice, at home and at the cosmopolitan level –

The History of the Human Species as a whole may be regarded as the unravelling of a hidden Plan of Nature for accomplishing a perfect state of Civil Constitution for Society ... as the sole State of Society in which the tendency of human nature can be all and fully developed.[48]

The aim may appear circular, but Kant believed he saw concrete proof of an upward movement towards its fulfilment, such

48. DEQUINCEY's translation in 1824, for the *London Magazine* of October of that year, reprinted in his *Collected Works* (ed. Masson, 1897), IX, 429, 439.

as the increase in liberty which could not be reversed, and the growth of enlightenment. Enlightened men will opt for the good, free men will refuse to be enslaved again by their rulers, and economic growth will make States more interdependent, and therefore less likely to go to war. A Universal History would help them to understand, and therefore speed their emancipation. His essay is kept at a high level of abstraction, with few references to concrete institutions except to note that Europe was leading in this development and was therefore likely to give laws to the rest. Nor is the 'Nature' which Kant places at the centre, clearly described: it might be Providential, Lamarckian, or Darwinian. But it is not difficult to see that the 'perfect civil union' which we are destined to reach is an abstraction of the Settlement of 1689, the Declaration of Independence, and the Declaration of the Rights of Man.

The optimism of Herder (1744–1803) was greater than Kant's in the same measure that Condorcet exceeded Turgot. In his *Ideas on the History of Humanity* (1784–91) he expressed the belief that human and social evolution will lead to the realization of higher potentialities, and further development of the human mind. He reduced the role played by Kant's reason and put his faith in nature, which was totally determinate and was carrying out *God's* purpose –

Everywhere that takes place which alone can take place, according to the position and need of place, the conditions and opportunities of time, and the innate or acquired character of nations.[49]

Even the appearance of a Luther is no accident –

... how many earlier Luthers arose in the past – and fell down again: their mouths stopped up with fire and smoke, or their words lacking the air of freedom in which they could be sounded – but now spring has come: the earth opens out, the sun burns down and a thousand new plants come forth – man, you were ever, almost against your will, but a small blind instrument.

49. HERDER, *Ideen zur Philosophie der Menschengeschichte*, in *Sämmtliche Werke* (ed. Suphan, Berlin, 1877–1913), XIV, 83.

Though we cannot see the whole design, we can get glimpses of it, and at best, realize that —

We are the scene of a directing intention of this earth.

All humanity is the purpose, and individuals are but the link in the great chain.

But he thought that the French *philosophes* had entirely misunderstood the nature of progress. It was not improvement in technology or commerce, for if they grew, something always declined. Nor was there any question of progress towards more virtue and happiness of the individual, for humanity is everywhere alike, and

there is in humanity an invisible germ of the capacity to enjoy happiness or act virtuously, all over the world and in every age, developed differently and appearing in different forms, but ever in only one measure, and one mixture of potency.

Progress was rather to be understood like the movement of a drop of water in a stream, the same drop, but ever going forward, inevitably to its destiny.[50]

Unfortunately, few of his ideas were fully worked out, and they exist only in the form of hints and flashes of insight, scattered about his work. One of the most fruitful of his thoughts concerns the relationship between the generalizing of natural laws as such, and the uniqueness of history, and between the general chain of history, and the all-embracing character and style of a period as such, in which he stands, as he stood temporarily, between the 'legal' mentality of the eighteenth century and the 'historical' of the nineteenth. Basing himself on Hume and the view that cause-effect relationships cannot be proved, but are merely acceptable to the mind and thus are philosophic rather than historical, he felt his way towards the later idealist position of looking for inner-spiritual, rather than pragmatic

50. *Auch eine Philosophie der Geschichte zur Bildung der Menschheit* (1774), op. cit., V, 532, 513, 558, 511, 558, 512.

relationships. Out of this arose his own peculiar contribution to historic thinking, the sympathetic sensing, or *Einfühlung* into an age.

Optimism was the key note also of Lessing's (1729–81) philosophy, but it was conceived in terms of the development of the human mind –

The human mind must pass through phases of ignorance, doubt, and even terror, before it can become capable of receiving pure truth.

Then, with self-education, it will understand the physical world of science and the divine scriptures, and men will perceive and do their moral duty. Mankind will enter upon its third age, adulthood, and will approach perfection and the highest grade of illumination and purity.[51]

A similar idealism, and similar preoccupation with the progress of the mind, dominate also the view on progress of Fichte (1762–1814) and Hegel (1770–1831). For both, progress occurred because of predetermined laws and not because of the wills of men themselves. Their notion that men's spirits were involuntary components of this inevitable upward sweep runs counter the Anglo-French conception, in which Providence and Progress are incompatible, and one had to die before the other could be sustained. It led the German idealists to make their most fruitful contributions to the question of freedom and free will in history. Fichte's freedom consists of the power of reason and the knowledge of the consequences of one's actions. The philosopher increasingly discovers the truths on which social progress depends, and since human progress is the highest moral aim, he will wish to apply them, thus ensuring both his own greater freedom, and mankind's progress. There is here no striving for happiness as an end, but of freedom and self-realization as the ideals which are always approached, but never reached. Hegel refined this idea further. Not only was the actual

51. LESSING, *The Education of the Human Race* (Transl. F. W. Robertson, 4th edn, 1896), pp. xiii, 68–70.

development of the world spirit not under the individual's control, but on the contrary, it caught up the individual in its relentless march forward. Freedom, however, the end to which this process was directed, consisted precisely in the recognition of the individual's impotence.

Hegel's view of history appears at first sight highly dynamic. History moves forward in great strides, fighting its battles as the heroes of its positive forward movement struggle with other great spirits who seem to oppose it, but whose opposition or 'antithesis', is equally historically justifiable and necessary for the emergence of a higher level, or 'synthesis', the next stage, when the process will begin again. Hegel's 'reason' or 'rationalism' in history, therefore, is very different from the mathematical reason or rationalism on which the natural sciences had been based up to that date, and it is from Hegel that much of the later metaphysical historiography draws its inspiration. Similarly, his insistence on taking the nation, or humanity, as the unit, which therefore became eternal and developing, while individuals were born and died, became a model for those who opposed the individualism of the economists. Yet in the end, Hegel's thought came to a conclusion which was static and not dynamic, and was used to support conservatism rather than progress. For Hegel saw the historical process largely as a political one, and the final state of freedom towards which the mountains of the historical world mind had laboured, was the Prussian Monarchy. Perhaps obedience to the commands of history merely meant obedience to the Prussian bureaucracy, after all.

All the German philosophers examined here kept to a high level of abstraction, and even their excursions into history tended to be analytical rather than descriptive of any particular time or place. Here, if anywhere, may we expect to find ideas pursued for their own sake, and unsullied by social reality. Yet here, too, the relation of the social bourgeois world picture to Kant or Lessing is only too plain, and Fichte threw himself with enthusiasm into the movement which first welcomed the French

Revolution as an end to absolutist and aristocratic obstruction, and later rallied the German middle classes against the French when the latter turned into conquering imperialists. By contrast, Hegel's view of history as a development up to the present, when it would come to a stop, having achieved perfection, was the stance natural to a class which has only recently come into its own, but is now basically satisfied and fears the rise of a class below it. It was appropriate to the Prussian squires and bureaucrats, looking back on a century of growth of their kingdom and their power, and for the same reason it could not be acceptable to the rising German bourgeoisie and lower middle classes, who therefore quickly transformed, in the 1830s and 1840s, the Hegelian dialectic into an engine of continuous progress.

Meanwhile, however, and particularly while the French Revolution was still shaking Europe, the forces of conservatism were fighting back vigorously, and using as their instrument the see-saw of ideas, the revulsion of each generation for the ideas of its fathers. Thus, in reaction against the rationalist absolutist standards of the Enlightenment, the new generation began to discover merit in the Middle Ages. In France, Catholic historians came back into their own. Everywhere in Europe, Romanticism captured the imagination of the creative artists. The Evangelical Revival arose to oppose the rule of reason and moderation; the growth of nationalistic feeling, particularly of the nations who had not achieved a modern independent State, opposed the cosmopolitanism of the *philosophes*; and the arts and personal accomplishments were valued more highly at the expense of the impersonal accumulation of scientific knowledge. The very excess of sobriety, of scientific objectivity, of reducing the role of the individual in the march of his generation, led to an excess in the opposite direction, and men like Carlyle (1795–1881) and William Roscoe (1753–1831) in Britain, Adam Müller (1779–1829) and Savigny (1779–1861) in Germany, and De Maistre (1753–1829) in France, could gain a respectful hearing once more.

It was inevitable, in the usual dialectic of ideas, that those who consciously set themselves to oppose one trend of thought, shared a good deal of its assumptions, so that much of the body of ideas of Enlightenment survived even among its opponents. Thus Wilhelm von Humboldt (1767–1835) carried over into his idealist history much of the speculative rationalism of the eighteenth century; thus the older Southey is still recognizably the same man as the young radical; and Madame de Staël (1766–1817), even while concentrating on one of the *lacunae* of the *savants*, the development of art, was not so much contradicting them as extending them, for she came to believe that while art, as they also had taught, could not advance beyond the capacity of each generation, human sensibility would widen with general progress, and there was a link between literature and social development.

Even the Romantic and conservative political reaction, the ideology of the old Europe which now began to hit back, could no longer shed all of the assumptions of the Enlightenment that had logically led to the American and French Revolutions. Burke (1729–97) is perhaps the best example here. He began his literary career with a satire, *A Vindication of Natural Society* (1756) which attempted to refute Bolingbroke by driving his ideas to extremes, and therefore required Burke to enter right into the spirit of the Enlightenment; he ended as the defender of conservatism and the bitterest enemy of the French Revolution only after long years of Whig politics, and support for the English and American Revolutions.

To Burke, men in the mass, social men, were irrational. Reason was useful, but experience was better, since reason was much more tied to its own specific age. What existed had proved its aptness, and any attempt at violent change was not only disruptive of society, but also doomed to failure. As in the case of all conservative thought of the 1790s, Burke ultimately holds continuity and social peace in much higher esteem than truth; and the common people may have to be lied to by their 'Trustees', their betters, for their own good, as the understanding of truth of every generation was bound to be limited.

Yet Burke represents not so much a denial of the Enlightenment as an enlargement of it. If he denies rationalism, and declares that men are in reality moved by passion rather than exclusively by reason, he accepts Utilitarianism and he uses history to learn what has made men happy in the past. If he believes that history never makes jumps, he also holds that individuals or the multitude may be wrong, though not mankind as a whole.

Changes do occur, and are ordained by God –

... we are in a manner compelled to acknowledge the hand of God in those immense revolutions, by which, at certain periods, He so signally asserts His supreme dominion, and brings about that great system of change, which is, perhaps, as necessary to the moral as it is found to be in the natural world.

The power of this divine determinism was absolute –

if a great change is to be made in human affairs, the minds of men will be fitted to it; the general opinions and feelings will draw that way. Every fear, every hope will forward it: and they who persist in opposing this mighty current in human affairs, will appear rather to resist the decrees of Providence itself, than the mere design of men. They will not be resolute and firm, but perverse and obstinate.[52]

For Burke, as for his opponents, the world progresses along a single track, and it is the crime of the French that they have made a schism with the whole universe. His complaint against it might have been echoed by any of the *philosophes* of the Enlightenment: he would be satisfied, he declared –

... When I shall learn, that in France, the Citizen ... is in a perfect state of legal security, with regard to his life, his property, to the uncontrolled disposal of his Person, to the free use of his Industry and his faculties; when I hear that he is protected in the beneficial Enjoyment of the Estates to which ... he was born; – that he is

52. *Abridgement of English History* (1757) and *Thoughts on French Affairs* (1791) in *Works* (ed. Fitzwilliam and Bourke, 8 vols., 1852), VI, 216, IV, 591.

maintained in the full fruition of the advantages belonging to [his] State and condition of life . . .; When I am assured that a simple Citizen may decently express his sentiments upon Publick Affairs, without hazard to his life or safety, even tho' against a predominant and fashionable opinion.[53]

The only striking thing is the lack of even the slightest sympathy for the French in trying to achieve this desirable state, Burke's much-praised 'Liberty', for themselves.

A hatred like Burke's has a personal element. It is not hard to see why a man like Burke, having risen by immense labour, and by incurring a dead weight of debt which was to press on his mind until death, from the position of a poverty-stricken scribe to a precarious foothold among the top rank of the landowning aristocracy, should heap such hatred and contempt upon the leaders of the Revolution. For they held up a distorted, yet recognizable mirror image of himself, several decades earlier, when a choice was still open to him. They had proved less financially successful no doubt, but their principles had proved stronger. In part, his fanaticism also arose from his belief that they were destroying a divinely ordained scheme of things. They were opposing themselves to social laws, which were not only 'natural' but had been willed by God. Finally, he was incensed by the insolence of the revolutionaries who dared to manipulate laws of modern society far too complex for their understanding –

Common wealths are not physical but moral essences. They are artificial combinations, and, in their proximate efficient cause, the arbitrary productions of the human mind. We are not yet acquainted with the laws which necessarily influence the stability of that kind of work made by that kind of agent. I doubt whether the history of mankind is yet complete enough, if it ever can be so, to furnish grounds for a sure theory on the internal causes which necessarily affect the fortunes of a State.[54]

53. *Letters on a Regicide Peace* (1796), in *Works*, V, 214–5; Letter to C. J. F. Depont, November 1789, in *Correspondence of Edmund Burke* (Cambridge, 1967), VI, 43.

54. *First Letter on a Regicide Peace* (1796), *Works*, V, 254.

In principle, Burke does not reject natural laws, neither does he reject individual free will in what is a determinate world. Man has an obligation to use the powers of reasoning, for God intended him to use them, and to make the best of his opportunities. Thus he has a right to attempt to improve his own social status, and even the conditions of his own society. What is, must be good, for God willed it, but He also willed us to improve it, and to make good, for example, the evils produced by the British occupation of India. God demands our cooperation. The unforgivable crime of the French Revolution, in Burke's eyes, was that it attempted to break out of God's law.

Thus Burke is, in many respects, in the Enlightenment tradition. There is evolution, and it is upwards and progressive, irreversible and inevitable, because ordained by Providence. The present society is greatly preferable to anything that went before – but, as was the case with all conservatives from Voltaire onwards, it is not nearly so evident that the future can bring further progress still. The reputation of Burke as the arch-conservative, compared with the iconoclasts of the generation preceding, is based largely on the fact that he had to observe what they merely discussed in theory: that history does at times make jumps.

Whatever the concrete economic, social and political origins of the French Revolution, there can be little doubt that its ideas had been shaped by the rational optimism of the Enlightenment. They dominated the leading defenders, and the leading opponents, of the convulsions that shook France and the whole of the Continent at the end of the century. These ideas, which included the idea of progress, survived as the heritage on which the nineteenth century, willingly or unwillingly, had to build its own philosophy.

CHAPTER THREE

THE NINETEENTH CENTURY:
THE HOPES OF LABOUR

THE Age of Innocence died with Condorcet. While some solitary souls still remained, after the Revolutionary and Napoleonic Wars, expecting miraculous changes from simple applications of such metaphysical concepts as 'Justice' or 'Natural Rights', the realists now knew that government by *philosophes*, by bourgeois, or even by the 'people' would not itself produce the millennium. Society was more complex than had been thought, and a new foundation had to be laid for a credible system of social laws.

Of course, the Revolution had symbolized a real shift of class power, and, both in France and in her occupied territories, the legal codes left behind furthered economic growth of the kind favoured by the bourgeoisie. If the flood of British manufactured imports after 1815 temporarily set back industrial and commercial developments in many countries, ultimately native entrepreneurship would create industrial revolutions in one area after another in the course of the century even in the teeth of British competition, and the promise of economic growth and scientific advance that had beckoned to the eighteenth century was kept. As a result, the idea of progress itself was held more widely, more strongly and more unselfconsciously than before.

In the earlier part of the century, all three leading systems of thought, nationalist liberalism, revolutionary socialism, and transcendent idealism, held to a doctrine of progress, even if for different reasons; while later on, Darwinism permeated every philosophy at least to the extent of postulating some process of evolution. Again, the hundred years' peace which saw the spread of industrial capitalism, and a vast increase in wealth in much of Europe and North America, gave renewed confidence to the bourgeoisie in its own future, within the existing social framework; yet at the same time the newly created proletariat transformed its early Utopian and Messianic hopes into a self-confident belief in its destiny, so that in this respect, too, the most diverse strands of interest could agree, at least, on the certainty of some 'progress'. Nineteenth-century man, as philosopher, as consumer, as member of a class, could accept the idea of progress almost as an axiom.

Characteristically, the most striking prophecy of progress which emerged out of the turmoil of the Revolution, that of Saint-Simon (1760–1825), was as many-sided and confused as the Revolution itself. For Saint-Simon's own thoughts went through several phases, promising in each the world to a different class, first to the *savants*, then to the *industriels* (by which term he originally meant the entrepreneurs), and finally to the proletarians. Accordingly, his doctrines have become the basis of such diverse phenomena as capitalist (particularly banking) enterprise, Socialism, and the intellectual's belief in a meritocracy.

Saint-Simon's literary career began in 1802, after forty-two packed years as privileged nobleman, as revolutionary adventurer, canal projector, land speculator and salon roué. His first booklet, *Lettres d'un habitant de Genève à ses contemporains* shows all his later characteristics of disordered exposition, violent language and occasional lapses into plain lunacy, but it is still very much in the Condorcet tradition. History for him is still essentially the history of ideas, and the dominant theme behind this conviction of progress was the expansion of science. But unlike the eighteenth-century *philosophes*, who saw the historical dynamic as arising out of pure science, Saint-Simon was more impressed by applied science, particularly by engineering, as taught at the new École Polytechnique. It was no accident that it was to be the *polytechniciens* who were later to become his disciples and who were, for good or ill, to turn Saint-Simonism into a doctrine of social engineering.

According to the *Lettres*, history consists of the development of the human spirit, and its progress derives from the work of individuals of genius, among 'des savants, des artistes et de tout les hommes qui ont des idées liberales'.[1] They should, therefore, hold the leading positions in the councils of the nations and in the 'temples of Newton', the mathematicians occupying the place of honour. In the *Essai sur l'organisation sociale*, the *Parlement de Perfectionnement* will consist of thirty *savants*, five artists and ten industrialists, presided over by a mathematician.[2] The details were to change many times in later publications, but Saint-Simon never lost the firm belief in government by the expert, chosen by his peers and elected by the nation at large. There were two reasons for this exaltation of the expert. The first was the consideration that, while the much-applauded politicans or generals benefit, at best, one part of humanity at the expense of the other, the scientist, engineer or artist, benefits mankind as a whole, and it is he who is the real author and creator of the progress of humanity. But secondly, now that social science itself was about to enter the stage at which the future could be foreseen to some extent, the expert could use his knowledge to make predictions. In a deeper sense, history is the march of progress laid down by God, and the object of human endeavour is to make human intelligence approach ever closer to divine foresight.

In virtually the whole of the eighteenth-century literature on progress, all practical proposals were designed to expand the opportunities open to the bourgeoisie. In the early Saint-Simon, this bias is subtly, but decisively changed. Social organization should be such as to provide opportunities for the carrier of the intellectual-moral progress himself: the professional, the intellectual, or the artist.

1. *Lettres* (1952, edn Alcan, Paris), pp. 10, 23.
2. Reprinted in ibid, p. 88.

This switch was to be of overwhelming significance in the further development of European thought. At one level, it opposed the *laissez-faire*, individualist, 'invisible hand' society, which was one of the ideals that had emerged in the eighteenth century, with the planned, organized, controlled, even totalitarian solution. It opposed to Liberalism, a form of State socialism and thereby set up the terms on which most of the Western world's political debates have been conducted to this day. At a deeper level, it opposed to the selfish interests of the owners of capital the selfish interests of the professional class, under a strikingly similar guise of making their special advancement a condition of the progress of all. The professional classes, however, in spite of much speculation about 'managerial revolutions' and the 'rise of the meritocracy', and in spite of a recent growth in numbers, could not be one of the main contenders in the social struggles of the past century and a half. Important though they are, they cannot impose their own version of progress, but have to side with one or the other of the two main contending classes. Those who, like Saint-Simon, were driven to join with the working classes, could henceforth do so under the banner of a *dirigiste*, expert-controlled State socialism.

The house of socialism has many rooms, and many different ideas have, at one time or another, sheltered under its roof. Socialism as a centrally planned, scientifically ordered society, is an idea which peculiarly favours the professional man, it is indeed his apotheosis, while neither in theory, nor even less in practice, has it turned out to be very much in favour of the working classes at the present stage of social development. Its leaders and prophets, not unnaturally, have everywhere been intellectuals and professional people. Working men, if left to themselves, tend to produce a very different blueprint of the future, in which, normally and not surprisingly, workshop self-government and some form of cooperative structure, of the direct opposite of State planning, occupy a leading place. Nevertheless, it is the recognizably Saint-Simonian type of socialism which has held the stage since his day, and still offers itself as the most credible alternative to capitalism at the present time.

If this picture of an organized, planned world, dealing with individuals with ruthless efficiency, was one solution to the miseries caused by anarchial capitalism that Saint-Simon fathered upon the working-class movement, he is responsible also for planting the seed of what is virtually the opposite ideal, the hope of substituting for the rule over man, the administration of things, and ending the 'exploitation of man by man' which characterized the capitalist and all earlier societies.[3] These sentiments, containing some of the noblest thoughts of the eighteenth century on the destiny of man, have survived the concrete social conditions in which they were born to become part of the Western heritage.

Saint-Simon's first phase ended about 1813. His *Réorganisation de la Société Européenne* of 1814 (written jointly with his disciple, Augustin Thierry) which contains proposals for a unified Europe built around an Anglo-French Alliance, still reserves, as all his works were to continue to do, a leading role for the scientists. But now they are joined by three other groups, and it is these four groups together who will be entitled to rule Europe because their work benefits the whole of the Continent: 'Des négotiants, des savants, des magistrats et des administrateurs'. Europe thus governed will extend the blessing of progress to the rest of the world, and set out to develop public works in Europe, and to 'populate the globe with the European race, which is superior to all human races, to make it accessible and habitable like Europe ...'

Thus the merchants and the bureaucracy have joined the scientists in 1814, but in the next six years or so the emphasis

3. This expression is found first among his disciples after his death, *The Doctrines of Saint-Simon: An Exposition. First Year 1828–1829* (Boston Mass. 1958), p. 64.

shifts to the '*industriels*'.[4] The term is neither quite clear nor quite stable in meaning, but in his famous 'parable' of 1819 [5] in which he contrasts the ease with which France could bear the loss of her thirty-nine thousand top politicians, generals, bishops, and proprietors, with the irreplaceable damage she would suffer if her top three thousand 'producers' were to die suddenly, he enumerates some sixty professions and occupations classed as productive. These range from doctors, scientists and artists to engineers, bankers, manufacturers and craftsmen, and a special footnote 'to avoid misunderstandings' makes it clear that he means farmers, traders, employers, clerks and workers. His hatred is reserved for the 'idle', who contribute nothing. Finally, from about 1820 onwards, Saint-Simon's hopes and interests centred increasingly upon 'la classe la plus nombreuse et la plus pauvre'.

While the limits of the class which would carry the progress of humanity during the next stage change in these important respects, basically the philosophy of Saint-Simon was centred from first to last on the belief in the inevitability of the progress of humanity. From one point of view, progress appears totally predestined –

At no period did the progress (*perfectionnement*) of civilization proceed along a path thought out and preconceived by a man of genius and adopted by the masses. This would be impossible even in the very nature of things, for the supreme law of progress of the human spirit carries along and dominates everything; men are but its instruments . . . it is no more in our power to withdraw ourselves from its influence or to control its action than it is to change at our pleasure the primitive impulse which makes our planet circle the sun. All we can do is to obey the law, by accounting for the course which it lays down for us, instead of being blindly pushed along by

4. Translation is difficult, as Saint-Simon attaches special meanings to some of these terms. *Oeuvres*, (6 vols., Paris, 1966), I, 199–200, 204.
5. *Organisateur*. Later reprinted separately as *Parabole de Saint-Simon*. *Oeuvres*, II, part 2, 17–26.

it; and, incidentally, it is precisely in this that the great philosophic development destined for the present era will consist.

There is a hint here that although we are being carried along an historic stream, the conclusions to be drawn are by no means fatalistic. In the first place, the mechanism is operated through human beings, and the motive force is the propensity of men to improve their condition –

Experience of all the known centuries has proved that mankind has always laboured towards the improvement of its fate and, consequently, towards perfecting its social organization, whence it follows that it is in its nature to improve indefinitely its political rule.

In the second place, and more significantly, the new science leaves a large, and a vital role, to the present generation. For this new science of society could not have arisen earlier –

First a system of social order has to be established, comprising a very numerous population and being composed of several nations, lasting over the whole possible period for that system, before a theory can be grounded on that great experience.

Only then can we be capable of 'distinguishing', as it were, at first glance, which improvements (*perfectionnements*) are part of the natural stages of development of the social state and which are not, and in what order.[6]

Thus a kindly Providence has provided a mechanism for progress by the working of the human instinct; but at the present stage, it required also conscious, informed collaboration from humanity, which has now been provided by Saint-Simon's science of society. Towards the end of his life, Saint-Simon came increasingly to believe both in a divine origin of that Providence, and in the need for religion to provide the social cohesion necessary for the next stage of advance. But as early as 1807–8 he expressed the opinion that 'Religion is the collection of applica-

6. 9th and 7th letters, ibid., II/2, 118,74. *Organisateur*, in *Oeuvres*, II/2, 8–9; Second letter, ibid., II/2, 31–2.

tions of general science by means of which enlightened men govern ignorant men'.[7]

Progress took place by a dialectical succession of 'organic' and 'critical' periods. In organic periods, all aspects of social life, all classes and all ideas, were in harmony and collaborated towards the common good. The world had seen two such periods, the classical Hellenic and the medieval Catholic, a third such period now being visible on the horizon. Asia and Africa were deliberately excluded, as having, at best, a single stage only to their credit. Critical periods, by contrast, were destructive of unity and harmony, and particularly in their later phases, in one of which Saint-Simon believed himself to be living, lost even the cohesion of attacking a common enemy. But these destructive phases were as necessary, as much part of the design for progress, as the happy periods of harmony: they carried the seeds of the next organic phase, as the organic phase had carried the seeds of its own destruction.

Saint-Simon had thus overcome one of the mental blocks of the Enlightenment which had failed to see any good in reactionary institutions or thought-inhibiting agencies like the Catholic Church. Up to the fifteenth century, indeed, during the second 'organic' period of humanity,

the men of the Church were superior to the laity in their talents and virtues. It was the clergy that cleared land for cultivation, and drained unhealthy marshes; it was they who deciphered ancient manuscripts. They taught reading and writing to the lay population . . . the clergy founded the first hospitals, and the first modern institutions of learning; they united the European nations in their resistance to the Saracens.

And again –

every religion begins as a beneficial institution. The priests abuse it when they are not held back by the constraints of an opposition,

7. *Introduction aux travaux scientifiques du XIXe siècle. Oeuvres*, VI, 169.

when they have no more scientific discoveries to make in the direction laid down by the founder: it then becomes oppressive.[8]

This more balanced view also immensely strengthened the hypothesis of perpetual progress, for the condemnation of the Middle Ages as a lapse from civilization had always left the objection that if there was one lapse, there could be others.

Each organic stage represented a distinct advance upon the last one, while each imposed its unitary character upon all aspects of society. Thus the first was characterized by polytheism and slavery, the second was theological and feudal, and the third, which was only then arising out of the critical chaos, would be positive and industrial. Under the influence of Comte, then acting as Saint-Simon's assistant, a further stage, the metaphysical and juridical was introduced between the last two. In the later writings, the last stage became increasingly the final, golden age, towards which mankind was moving, a heaven on earth.

This development conceals a more significant shift. The early Saint-Simon, we noted above, followed Condorcet in seeing progress as a development of the mind. As late as 1813 he could write that 'Systems of religion, of general politics, morality, of public instruction, are nothing else than applications of a system of ideas.' But in his 'positive' phase, the influence is not entirely in one direction; on the contrary, he sees concrete events, such as the French Revolution, determining systems of thought. Again, his later plans envisage the replacement of the military classes by the 'peaceful' and 'industrial' classes as the ruling elements in society, and he was much concerned with the political status and the economic rewards of the 'industrial' and working classes. Ideology, the system of thought, would then reflect social organization, and the coming organic period is as much a phase of social organization (or 'universal association', as his disciples were to term it) as a phase of positive science.

8. *Oeuvres*, VI, pp. 161–2, 169.

Finally, this switch towards materialism was also reflected in his teleology. The end towards which mankind progresses is not only perfect knowledge, or morality, or even freedom. Science would benefit humanity also because it would raise the standard of living of the masses. One class replaces another, the industrialists replace the feudalists, because they are more efficient at producing wealth –

The production of useful things is the only reasonable and positive end that political scenes can set themselves ... The producers of useful things being the only useful people in society, are the ones who should collaborate to regulate its course.

In the new political order, social organization will have for its sole and permanent purpose the best possible use for the satisfaction of human needs of all the knowledge acquired in the sciences, the fine arts, and industry.[9]

In spite of the ill-organized nature of Saint-Simon's works (or perhaps because of it) he managed to originate a staggering number of new thoughts developed out of the heritage of the eighteenth century, and influencing the thought and the history of the nineteenth. He predicted correctly not only the growth of industry and of capitalism – there were many others who could see so far – but he also turned out to be right in envisaging the vast growth of the bureaucracy and the professional classes and white-collar workers, and the corresponding growth of social control associated with it; the expansion of European enterprise into the rest of the world; and despite the difference from the only model he could have observed, the British economy, the key role to be played by bank finance, and centrally planned public utilities, the significance of which has only recently come home to us. He was among the first to relate the ideology of each age to its dominant class system, and to judge institutions, ideas

9. *Mémoire sur la science de l'homme* (1813), *Oeuvres* V/2, 18; *L'Industrie* (1817), Vol. 1, Part 2 in *Oeuvres*, I/2, 186–7; *L'Organisateur* (11th letter), *Oeuvres* II/2, 193.

and religions not by any absolute standard, but by their relevance to their own stage of progress, and thus became a forerunner of historicism as well as of materialism. He developed the stage theory and, before the influence of Hegel had spread across Europe, made the mode of his progress dialectical as the alteration of organic and critical phases, as he had earlier seen the advance of science, alternatively synthesizing (that is putting the theory first) and analysing (that is putting facts first). Last, but not least, his were among the first modern expressions of socialism.

After his death his disciples formed a sect which had at one time perhaps as many as forty thousand adherents, and counted among its leaders some of the most influential men of the next generation. In the hands particularly of Enfantin (1796–1864) and Bazard (1791–1832), the religious side of Saint-Simon's teaching was developed further, ultimately to sectarian heights which embarrassed most of their sympathizers, and the emphasis on just treatment of the working classes and on State control of the economy became stronger. In a series of lectures, published as *Doctrines of Saint-Simon*, they succeeded in making the doctrine more systematic and internally consistent than it had been left by the master.

For them, progress was even more certain than for Saint-Simon, if that were possible –

The most general fact in the growth of societies, the one which implicitly includes all the others, is the progress of the moral conception by which man becomes conscious of a social destiny.

Indeed –

The law of perfectibility is so absolute, it is a condition so deeply bound up with the condition of our species, that whenever a people at the end of humanity becomes static, the germs of progress within it are immediately carried elsewhere to a soil where they can be developed.

This view, though apparently more definite, yet leaves more to chance and to mystical hope than did the master, or the Saint-Simonian emissaries to England, Fontana and Prati. For them, each stage develops inevitably out of the previous one, and it is impossible to halt history or put back the clock. If one wanted to restore feudalism, for example, one would have to restore serfdom, and even then history would repeat the same events leading out of it, for it was 'impossible to extinguish the system of progressive civilization' which the Deity had decreed for the whole family of man –

History . . . presents a successive table of the physiological states of the human species, considered in its collective existence. Indeed, it constitutes a science which takes in the rigorous character of the exact sciences.[10]

But the disciples are less certain about the mechanism, and therefore have to bring in God. Of the three 'aspects' of man, feeling, or human sympathy, is the static factor, but the other two, intellect and material activity, are the progressive elements, one representing the idealist, the other the materialist cause of progress. Despite this apparent double causation, it is likely that for the Saint-Simonians it was the spirit that was primary, and the political and social relations of each age are the expressions of its 'idea'. Man is moved by 'sympathy', which comes from God, and the world is so designed that this sympathy will make us perform acts which will ensure human progress.

But if the mechanism is mysterious, the course of future history is clear. There will be ever widening 'association', from the family, to the city, the nation state, and in the future, the whole world; and from limited functional association to association in all aspects of life, 'universal association'. 'The successive development of the human species recognizes only one single law, the uninterrupted progress of association': this will mark the third

10. *Doctrines of Saint-Simon*, pp. 28, 32, 36; R. K. P. PANKHURST, *The Saint Simonians, Mill and Carlyle* (1957), p. 102.

organic period. In place of antagonism, 'physical force and the exploitation of man by man', 'this development [of mankind] may be expressed in the constant growth of the rule of love, harmony, and peace', shown already by such developments as the evolution of slavery, via serfdom, to the wage system. Similarly, in the critical periods, particularly towards their end,

the men who figure in it … preach hatred through love; call for destruction while believing to be building … Let us pity them … for having been given the terrible mission which they have fulfilled with devotion and love for mankind. Let us pity them, for they were born to love and their entire life was dedicated to hate.

The next stage of universal associations was not final –

We do not say that mankind, once it has reached this state, will no longer have any progress to make. On the contrary, it will march faster than ever towards perfection. But this epoch will be final for mankind in the sense that it will have realized the political combination most favourable to progress … the fields of science and industry will gather daily more abundant harvests and will furnish man with new ways to express his love ever more nobly. He will broaden the sphere of his intelligence, that of his physical power, and that of his sympathies, for the course of his progress is unlimited.[11]

This doctrine compared with the Enlightenment in its power to unite large numbers of dedicated men, and to influence a whole generation. Both movements promised progress on this earth, and based it on science and reason: perhaps Ernest Renan's *L'Avenir de la Science* (1848) was the clearest expression of that optimism. But in contrast with the Enlightenment, the bearer of the reason of humanity was not the moderate, thoughtful individual, but a whole class, increasingly identified as the working class, and the end of the historical process was not the liberation of the human mind, but the rational, purposeful organization of society, although ultimately this organization

11. *Doctrines*, pp. 38–9, 4, 59–61, 63–4, 87–8, 208–9, 69.

also had as its end the liberation and development of the individual.

The strand in Saint-Simon which placed the history of mind supreme in world history, was carried a stage further by Auguste Comte (1798–1857), an early disciple who quickly turned against and denied the master. The basic similarities may be discerned from the daily incantation prescribed by Comte for humanity in his later religious stage: 'L'amour pour principe, l'ordre pour base, et le progrès pour but'; but Comte saw all history as developing in three stages of thought. The first, 'theological' or fictitious stage, corresponds to the primitive assumption that all unexplored phenomena have a supernatural origin; the second, 'metaphysical' or 'abstract' stage, which began about the year 1400, corresponds to the attempt by philosophers to make norms of qualities, and to believe that these 'entities of personified abstractions' have some kind of independent existence, and the third, 'positive' or scientific stage, is the one which Comte believed himself to be ushering in in Europe, and in relation to the social sciences. Compared with the rich and fertile, though disorganized imagination of Saint-Simon, Comte's thought was narrow, but well structured, and can be found in two large works, carefully and meticulously organized, the *Cours de philosophie positive* (1830–42) and the *Système de politique positive* (1852–4). Similarly, while Saint-Simon's knowledge was limited and often hazy, Comte laboured with immense erudition to prove, not only that each science went separately through its three stages, but that there was a progressive hierarchy of sciences, beginning with mathematics and astronomy and rising, via physics and chemistry, to biology and sociology, and towards the highest science, ethics.

The driving force behind the inevitability of the advance of the human mind is, as for Saint-Simon, man's tendency to act upon nature and to modify it to his advantage. In science, this drive leads to the discovery of even more 'laws', or general regularities of relationships between single phenomena, and these diminish as the sciences advance, to create ultimately a single corpus of understanding of the universe. This concept, an attempt to match Newtonian 'gravity' or 'attraction', is already to be found in Saint-Simon's *Mémoire sur la science de l'homme* of 1813, as well as in Proudhon. In term of social action, the desire leads to the successions of changes which make up human history.

Social science may be divided into statics and dynamics, the counterparts of order and progress, or of stability and innovation, which make society both predictable and progressive. Social statics studies the interaction, in a given logical system, of all the component parts of a social organism on each other. 'There must always be a spontaneous harmony between the whole and the parts of the social system.' In particular, each stage of mental development is appropriate to its society, and must not be judged in any other terms. Polytheism, for example, was appropriate to antiquity, and therefore in the long-term view, progressive, and monotheism to the Middle Ages (both were stages of the theological phase), while positivism corresponds to the needs of modern industry; and the attack on religion by the metaphysicians corresponds to the political and economic undermining of feudalism.

Social dynamics studies the methods and sequences of change. Change from one system to the next may be disorderly, but it is necessary; the purpose of political action is to bring it about and the leaders are those who have correctly perceived the needs of the time. 'In politics, as in science, *opportuneness* is always the main condition of all great and durable influence.' To suggest the opposite, that great men make history, is to neglect the enormous disproportion between the alleged cause and effect –

Such an error is exactly of the same nature as that of the Indians who attributed to Christopher Columbus the eclipse which he had foreseen.

The role of the great individual lies

in the intelligent apprehension of these laws through observation, his forecast of their effects, and the power which he thus obtains of subordinating them to the desired end, provided he employs them in accordance with their nature.[12]

Each consecutive social state is 'the necessary result of the preceding, and the indispensable mover of the following, according to the axiom of Leibniz – "the present is big with the future".' But the nascent positive phase has a particularly progressive character –

Industrial life is at bottom in direct contradiction with all providential optimism, since it necessarily assumes that the order of nature is so imperfect as to require incessant amendment by man.

While the thought processes of metaphysics and theology do not lend themselves to a continuous progress towards a distant goal, 'progress at the present day is nowhere so manifest as in the whole range of scientific studies'.[13] Further, in his schematic view of the sciences, each science adds some new principle in emerging from the science below it, and the new element added by sociology is the historical method. Sociological 'facts' were distinguished from others by being historical.

Comte's claim was that it was he who had lifted sociology, or analytical history, up to its third stage as a positive science, and with it had made all knowledge truly scientific. It would, therefore now be possible to predict the future on the basis of known social laws, and for this power, Comte relied heavily on statistics. Basing himself in part on the work of the Belgian, Quetelet (1796–1874), particularly his book *Sur l'homme* (1835), he

12. HARRIET MARTINEAU, *The Positive Philosophy of Auguste Comte, Freely Translated and Condensed* (1853, 2nd ed. 1875), pp. 65, 77; 'Politics and Society' (1822), in PATRICK GARDINER, *Theories of History* (Glencoe, Ill., 1959), p. 81.

13. MARTINEAU, p. 69; COMTE, *A Discourse on the Positive Spirit* (1844, Eng. edn 1903), pp. 52, 92.

showed that there were striking regularities even in such apparently haphazard actions as suicides or accidents, and this application of the theory of probability to social facts, impressively supported by Mill, became one of the main foundations of the confidence of social scientists in the nineteenth century.

The progress of the human mind was undoubtedly at the centre of Comte's considerations. 'We must . . . preserve the general history of the human mind as the natural guide to all historical study of humanity.' Yet he also envisaged a necessary and concomitant advance in the arts, in customs and manners, in social organization, and ultimately also in man's mental and moral faculties. Much good will come from the mere fact of social order and collaboration, and from the transfer of political decisions, from selfish competition to the impartial science of the experts –

The metaphysical order sanctioned egotism; and the theological subordinated real life to an imaginary one, while the new philosophy takes social morality for the basis of its whole system.[14]

Even Comte, however, was driven by his preoccupation with social evolution to relax the uncompromising primacy of the mind over historical development. Thus, while man's action on his environment depends on the state of his knowledge, and history consists of the growing extent of his control over it, 'all human progress, political, moral, or intellectual, is inseparable from material progression.' And in dealing with concrete history, Comte designates the emancipation of the serfs

the greatest temporal evolution ever experienced by mankind, since its direct effect was to change irrevocably the natural mode of existence.

The key inventions, like the compass, firearms and printing were 'the result of the state of contemporary society'; the 'industrial' phase would develop human faculties more than the

14. MARTINEAU, pp. 130, 461–2.

'military' phase of history; and even the basis of art is to be found in its changing historical and social setting.[15]

The influence of Comte went deep, if not very wide, and extended via Mill, Buckle and George Eliot to Veblen and L. T. Hobhouse into the twentieth century. He laid the foundations of a scientific sociology, having the laws of social change as its objective. As far as the impact on the ideology of real classes was concerned, however, he found the bourgeoisie not at all anxious for further change, and applauding instead the conservative historians who preached reaction, legitimacy, and rights based on mystical prescription. He appealed less directly to the professional's interest than did Saint-Simon, and in spite of the sharp social criticism, he offered little comfort to the working classes.

The dilemma of John Stuart Mill (1806–73) was that he attempted to bridge in his philosophy the two disparate, almost incompatible streams into which eighteenth-century optimism had been divided: the individualist libertarian defence of the social *status quo*, associated particularly with the economists and the Utilitarians, and the progressive urge to engineer further social change by means of greater central social control. Brought up rigidly by his great Utilitarian father to the former doctrine, his own personal crisis, described movingly in his *Autobiography*, consisted in part in embracing much of the latter, under the influence first of the Saint-Simonians and later of Comte.

Mill, like Turgot, Condorcet and Comte, believed that the course of history was determined by ideas –

> The evidence of history and that of human nature combine, by a striking instance of consilience, to show that there is a social element which is predominant, and almost paramount, among the agents for social progression. That is, the state of the speculative faculties of mankind; including the nature of the beliefs which ... they have arrived at concerning themselves and the world by which they are surrounded.

15. MARTINEAU, pp. 98, 311, 319, 312, 330.

Social change occurs if 'the old order has become unsuited to the state of society and of the human mind'. Elsewhere, he compares the intellect to the steersman of the ship of history –

It is the steerman's will and the steerman's knowledge which decide in what direction it shall move.[16]

This gives us the power to control our destinies, since they are ruled by the intellect and by knowledge which are in our power.

What impressed Mill particularly in the doctrines of the Saint-Simonians was

the connected view which they for the first time presented to me, of the natural order of human progress; and especially with their division of all history into organic periods and critical periods.

This was vital for the would-be reformer who would have to, as he confided to his Saint-Simonian correspondent, d'Eichthal, in 1829,

ascertain what is the state into which, in the natural order of the advancement of civilization, the nation in question will next come.

It is true that he also voiced his misgivings at the rigidity of the Frenchman's pattern, and asserted that

different nations, indeed different minds, may and do advance to improvement by different roads,

but d'Eichthal was able to agree to this up to a point –

mais aujourd'hui c'est le phénomène le plus général qu'il nous faut d'abord étudier.[17]

In Comte, Mill admired in addition the heritage of Hume and Bentham, the belief in the power of rational thought, and the

---

16. *System of Logic* (8th edn, 1900), pp. 604–5. The key passages are reprinted in GARDINER, op. cit., pp. 83 ff; see also *The Spirit of the Age* (1831; Chicago, 1942), p. 6; *Auguste Comte and Positivism* (4th edn, 1891), pp. 104–5.

17. *Autobiography* (1873), p. 163; I. W. MUELLER, *John Stuart Mill and French Thought* (Urbana, Ill., 1956), pp. 58–9.

concept of progress of humanity as a living being, surviving while its individual members were born and died. The key concept for Mill was the conversion of sociology, and therefore also history, into a science. Mill grappled with this problem most seriously in his *System of Logic* (1843). Combining Comte's social statics and social dynamics, he arrived at the position that

the fundamental problem of the social science, is to find the laws according to which any state of society produces the state which succeeds it and takes its place.

In the question of the unpredictable influence of individuals on history

what science can do is this. It can trace through past history the general causes which had brought mankind into that preliminary state, which, when the right sort of great man appeared, rendered them accessible to his influence ... It is in this manner that the results of progress, except as to the celerity of their productions, can be, to a certain extent, reduced to regularity and law.

Since it is society as a whole which determines the shape of the whole of society of the next generation

rather than any part a part ... little progress ... can be made in establishing the filiation directly for laws of human nature, without having first ascertained the immediate or derivative laws according to which social states generate one another as society advances – the *axiomata media* of General Sociology.

There is 'a certain degree of uniformity in the progressive development of the Species and its works', becoming greater as civilization advances, as nations react more and more on each other. 'History, accordingly does, when judiciously examined, afford Empirical Laws of Society.'[18]

The support for Comte is there, but it is circumscribed, and as Mill grew older, his misgivings about Comte's certainties

18. *System of Logic*, pp. 595, 613, 603, 597–8.

increased. History, he felt, only had 'empirical', not scientific laws, based on less analytical understanding than those of the physical sciences. Moreover, he grew increasingly impatient with Comte's authoritarianism, his quasi-religious fantasies, and his emphasis on the finality of 'positive' science and of the next historical stage. At the same time, the other side of Mill, his Benthamism, reasserted itself: besides the laws of change affecting whole societies, there was also the very different thought world of political economy with its eternal constants of human psychology –

The succession of states of the human mind and of human society cannot have an independent law of its own; it must depend on the psychological and ethological laws which govern the action of circumstances on men and men on circumstances.

If a law of progress emerges from this, then it is a derived law derived from the science of psychology. General sociology has to combine the laws of social change 'with the laws of human nature'.

Thus, out of the interaction of two sets of laws, arises the complex nature of historical science, requiring the special 'inverse deductive', or historical method of investigation –

The principal cause of this peculiarity is the extensive and constant reaction of the effects upon their causes. The circumstances in which mankind are placed, operating according to their own laws and to the laws of human nature, from the character of human beings, but the human beings, in their turn mould and shape the circumstances for themselves and for those who come after them.

Political economists were falsely accused of considering one type of economy only, the European: they knew quite well that they were dealing with one type of many. But they were rightly attacked for basing their laws on eternal human nature, whilst human beings were also formed by their past history to an extent which allows us to derive laws of historical development.[19]

19. *System of Logic*, pp. 597, 598, 595–6; *August Comte and Positivism*, pp. 81–5.

Thus, against Comte, he held the idea of individual freedom and the dynamic of individual initiative, that were the cornerstone of the economists; and against the latter, he upheld the historians' emphasis of the changing social framework –

It was partly by [the Saint-Simonians'] writings that my eyes were opened to the very limited and temporary value of the old political economy, which assumes private property and inheritance as indefatigable facts, and freedom of production and exchange as the *dernier mot* of social improvement.

Yet he never emancipated himself fully from the classical view. It is true that he stressed that the role of the State cannot be determined in the abstract, but must depend on the stage of development and the kind of society, and that it would commonly and rightly be larger than in nineteenth-century Britain. But he was unable quite to shake off the Ricardian belief in future material stagnation, as improved industrial technology would be neutralized by ever rising real costs in agriculture, despite accelerating 'unlimited growth of man's power over nature'.[20] The danger was that the great mass of the people might, as always, remain near the subsistence level, and much of his work was devoted to problems of 'distribution', that is a fairer share-out of society's product, rather than with the consequences of ever-rising material prosperity. The only issue on which Comte and the political economists could fully and happily agree was their common assurance that the next stage of progress would be led by the bourgeoisie.

The two great streams into which the progressive philosophy had become divided in the nineteenth century, could each be pressed into service by the two main emerging social classes, capital and labour. The *dirigiste*, organized, scientific and planned social ideal, could be used, via Comte, by the middle classes in certain countries, and, via some of the Saint-

20. *Autobiography*, pp. 166–7; *Principles of Political Economy* (1896 edn), pp. 575–91, 422.

Simonians, it became the basis of modern socialism as a working-class ideology. The opposite anarchic, free, private enterprise doctrine had become, in the hands of British political economy, the ideology of the capitalist class. Mill straddled unhappily all these categories, but came closer than anyone else to the fourth possible combination, free enterprise in the interest of the labouring class. After condemning, in the first edition of his *Principles of Political Economy*, both Owenite socialism and continental communism, a striking change was introduced into the third edition (1852), where he thought it possible that ultimately one or other of these two systems would combine 'the greatest personal freedom with a just distribution of the fruits of labour', and in any case he

felt that the proclamation of such an ideal of human society, could not but tend to give a beneficial direction to the efforts of others to bring society, as at present constituted, nearer to some ideal standard.[21]

His own preference was for the cooperative, that is decentralized, rather than planned socialist economy, but by the end of his life his support even for that ideal had become lukewarm, except as a long-term aim to be reached after moral and intellectual regeneration of the whole population, and he was then even more hostile to centrally planned socialism.

The age of Mill was the last which could discuss the validity of social theories in generalized terms, as if every thinker and his public were concerned only with eternal values. It was in this period that a new understanding of the social dynamic was first offered, which set out to show that all ideas are but the reflection, in intellect and consciousness, of the social actions, the struggles and tensions, in which human beings, grouped in classes, engage in society. As Marx (1813–83) and his life-long collaborator, Engels (1820–95), claimed to have absorbed the finest components of progressive Western thought, German philo-

21. *Autobiography*, p. 167.

sophy, French socialism and British political economy, as well as, beyond dispute, the Enlightenment from which the others derived, so in turn their own conception of human history and social destiny henceforth was to dominate much that was best in progressive Western thought. As interpreters and guides of the historical process they are widely held to be in a class by themselves.

In their youth they had been deeply influenced by the two reactions against Hegel then current among the young spirits of Germany: the attempt of the Young Hegelians to turn the Hegelian dialectic from a defence of the Prussian Monarchy, into a handmaiden of progressive, even socialist thought; and the attempt by others, such as Feuerbach, to counter idealism and religious superstition by a crude materialism. But while both of them were still in their twenties, they had worked out their own reply, dynamic, or as they preferred to call it, dialectical materialism.

At the centre of their historical view was man as a social animal, in the setting of his real world, surviving by maintaining relations with other men in society. The key factors thus were man's material needs, food, shelter, clothing, and the form of social organization for providing them. Since man is a conscious being, he will develop ideas about his environment, his society and his history, but not in a vacuum; he will develop them in the process of acting out his part in history.

The German idealists or so-called 'true' socialists are criticized for considering

foreign communist literature not as an expression and the product of a real movement but merely as a set of theoretical writings. It has been evolved, they imagine, by 'pure thought', after the fashion of the German philosophical systems. It never occurs to them that even when these writings do preach a system, they spring from the practical needs, the whole conditions of life of a particular class in a particular country.

The ultimate causes of all social changes and political revolutions are to be sought, not in the minds of men, in their increasing insight into eternal truth and justice, but in changes in the mode of production and exchange; they are to be sought not in the *philosophy* but in the *economics* of the period concerned.

It is not the consciousness of men that determines their existence, but, on the contrary, their social existence that determines their consciousness. . . . This consciousness must . . . be explained from the contradictions of material life, from the existing conflict between the social forces of production and the relations of productions . . . Mankind always takes up only such problems as it can solve; since looking at the matter more closely, we will always find that the problem itself arises only when the material conditions necessary for its solution already exist or are at least in the process of formation.[22]

Turning to the other flank, by contrast –

The chief defect of all hitherto existing materialism is that the thing, reality, sensuousness, is conceived only in the form of the *object* or of *contemplation*, but not as human *sensuous activity*, *practice*, not subjectively . . . The materialist doctrine that men are products of circumstances and upbringing, and that, therefore, changed men are products of other circumstances and changed upbringing forgets that it is men that change circumstances and that the educator himself must be educated . . . Social life is essentially *practical* . . . the philosophers have only *interpreted* the world in various ways; the point however is to change it.[23]

Thus the role of the individual in history is to act, and in acting,

22. MARX and ENGELS, *The German Ideology* (1845–6, London, 1942 edn), p. 79; ENGELS, *Anti-Dühring* (1878, London, 1943 edn), p. 294. MARX, *A Contribution to the Critique of Political Economy* (1859, Chicago, 1913 edn), pp. 11–13. It has often been noted that after the failure of the 1848 Revolution, and the failure of the bulk of the working classes to embrace Marxism in the following three decades, the authors came increasingly to stress the false consciousness and ideology over true consciousness, and the underlying economic evolution over ephemeral political struggles; e.g. LEONARD KRIEGER, 'Marx and Engels as Historians', *J. Hist. Id.*, 14 (1953).

23. MARX, *Thesis on Feuerbach* (jotted down 1845).

to think, to will, and to create both his own history and his own thought about history, which will, in turn, influence the way he acts out his historic role.

Engels had to admit later –

Marx and I are ourselves partly to blame for the fact that younger writers sometimes lay more stress on the economic side than is due to it. We had to emphasize this main principle in opposition to our adversaries, who denied it, and we had not always the time, the place or the opportunity to allow the other elements involved in the interaction to come into their rights.

Their real views were more complex and less easy to summarize –

According to the materialist conception of history the determining element in history is *ultimately* the production and reproduction in real life. More than that neither Marx nor I have ever asserted ... The economic situation is the basis, but the various elements of the superstructure – political forms of the class struggle and its consequences, constitutions established by the victorious class after a successful battle, etc. – forms of law – and then even the reflexes of all these actual struggles in the brains of the combatants: political, legal, philosophical theories, religious ideas ... also exercise their influence upon the course of the historical struggles and in many cases preponderate in determining their *form*. There is an interaction of all these elements in which, amid all the endless *hosts* of accidents (i.e. of things and events whose inner connection is so remote or impossible to prove that we regard it as absent and can neglect it), the economic movement finally asserts itself as necessary ... We make our own history, but in the first place under very definite presuppositions and conditions. Among these the economic ones are finally decisive.[24]

The political superstructure is, of course, particularly important –

On the whole, the economic movement gets its way, but it has also to suffer reactions from the political movement which it

24. Letter to J. Bloch, 21 Sept. 1890, in MARX and ENGELS, *Selected Correspondence 1846–1895* (London, 1941 edn), pp. 475–7.

established and endowed with relative independence itself . . . The reaction of the state power upon economic development can be one of three kinds; it can run in the same direction, and the development is more rapid; it can oppose the line of development, in which case nowadays state power in every great nation will go to pieces in the long run, or it can cut off the economic development from certain paths, and impose it on certain others . . . it is obvious that in cases two and three the political power can do great damage to the economic development and result in the squandering of great masses of energy and material.

The law, also, reflects economic reality, but may modify it –

even religion and philosophy, by the very falsity of their conception of nature, react back on society, and so does science, even as it approaches ever closer to reality. After all, 'why do we fight for the political dictatorship of the proletariat if political power is economically impotent? Force [that is State power] is also an economic power'.[25]

When, therefore, it is a question of investigating the driving forces which – consciously or unconsciously, and indeed very often unconsciously – lie behind the motives of men in their historical actions and which constitute the real ultimate driving forces of history, then it is not a question so much of the motives of single individuals, however eminent, as of those motives which set in motion great masses, whole peoples, and again whole classes of people . . . not momentarily . . . but for a lasting action resulting in a great historical transformation. To ascertain the driving causes which here in the minds of acting masses and their leaders . . . are reflected as conscious motives – that is the only path which can put us on the track of the laws holding sway both in history as a whole, and at particular periods and in particular lands.

However obscure the mechanism may have been in the past –

. . . since the establishment of large-scale industry . . . it has been no longer a secret to any man in England that the whole political

25. *Correspondence.* Letter to Conrad Schmidt, 27 Oct. 1890, pp. 480–84.

struggle there has turned on the supremacy of two classes, the landed aristocracy and the middle class. In France, with the return of the Bourbons, the same fact was perceived ... And since 1830 the working class, the proletariat, has been recognized in both countries as a competitor for power ... In modern history at least it is therefore proved that all political struggles are class struggles, and all class struggles for emancipation in the last resort, despite their necessarily political form ... turn ultimately on the question of *economic* emancipation. Therefore, here at least, the state – the political order – is the subordinate, and civil society, the realm of economic relations – the decisive element.[26]

We therefore have here, in general terms, an irresistible engine of social progress, deriving from the conditions of each stage the necessity of the emergence of the next stage, the result of apparently blind forces, yet at the same time conscious, purposeful human action which can be described so that it makes sense, and which can ultimately be predicted.

Marx and Engels accepted the Saint-Simonian distinction between relatively stable, equilibrium periods, and periods of rapid change. But the latest, bourgeois or capitalist stage, while conforming to the general pattern in many essentials, for example in representing a form of exploitation of one class by another and in having its dominance settled by a violent political upheaval, represented a decisively new phase of world history. In part, its unique role derived from its vastly enhanced productive powers of society and the material wealth that could be made available, and in part from its highly restless, progressive, innovating, expansive and conquering nature, to the description and explanation of which Marx devoted his major work, *Das Kapital*.

This historical role of capitalism, which we are beginning to understand fully only today, was strikingly foreseen, almost a century and a quarter ago, in the *Communist Manifesto* written in a white heat of enthusiasm towards the end of 1847 –

26. FRIEDRICH ENGELS, *Ludwig Feuerbach and the Outcome of Classical German Philosophy* (1888, Engl. edn, Moscow 1946), pp. 58–61.

The bourgeoisie ... has accomplished wonders far surpassing Egyptian pyramids, Roman aqueducts, and Gothic cathedrals, it has conducted expeditions that put in the shade all former Exoduses of nations and crusades ... It has created more massive and more colossal productive forces than have all preceding generations together ... The need of a constantly expanding market for its products drives the bourgeoisie over the whole surface of the globe ... by the rapid improvement of all instruments of production, by the vastly easier means of communication [it] draws all, even the most barbarian, nations into civilization ... It compels them to introduce what it calls civilization into their midst, i.e. to become bourgeois themselves. In one word, it creates a world after its own image.

So much might have been foreseen also by the more perceptive of the political economists, from whom Marx learnt most of what he knew of the analysis of the capitalist economic system. Also, they would have agreed that

A country in which industrial development is more advanced than in others, simply presents those others with a picture of their own future.[27]

But the economists stopped there, thinking capitalism to be the end-product of history. They

have a singular method of procedure. There are only two kinds of institutions for them, artificial and natural. The institutions of feudalism are artificial institutions, those of the bourgeoisie are natural institutions ... [By this, they] imply that ... these relations are themselves ... eternal laws which must always govern society. Thus there has been history, but there is no longer any.

The moment the bourgeoisie has smashed the old society and its apparatus of power, 'the revolutionary class becomes conservative'.

But with its victory, the bourgeoisie has, in turn, called into

27. From the Preface to the First German edition of *Kapital* (1867, Everyman's edn 1929), p. 863.

being its own oppressed class, its grave-diggers, the proletariat, and this develops its own view of society –

... Just as the *economists* are the scientific representatives of the bourgeoisie class, so the *Socialists* and the *Communists* are the theoreticians of the proletarian class.

In the early stages they are merely Utopians; but as the proletariat develops

they have only to take note of what is happening before their eyes and to become the mouthpiece of this ... From this moment, science ... has ceased to be doctrinaire, and has become revolutionary.[28]

What of the proletariat's vision of progress, as expressed on its behalf by Marx and Engels? There is some justification for the statement that they saw the next, and last, proletarian Revolution in apocalyptic terms, when 'the knell of capitalist private property sounds; the expropriators are expropriated',[29] after which history as we know it would cease. Here is, for example, Engels' preface to the 1888 edition of the *Manifesto* –

... the whole history of mankind (since the dissolution of primitive tribal society, holding land in common ownership) has been a history of class struggles ... the history of these class struggles forms a series of evolutions in which nowadays, a stage has been reached in which the exploited and oppressed class – the proletariat – cannot attain its emancipation ... without, at the same time, and once and for all emancipating society at large from exploitation, oppression, class distinction and class struggles.

Marx envisaged, after the socialist society, which will bear the marks of its capitalist origins, at least one other stage, the

28. MARX, *The Poverty of Philosophy* (1847, English edn 1941), pp. 102, 104, 106–7. In 1888, Engels was to write in a preface to a new edition of the *Communist Manifesto* that 'in 1847, Socialism was a middle-class movement, Communism a working-class movement'. The groups are described in some detail in the *Manifesto*.

29. *Kapital*, p. 846.

higher phase of communist society, after the enslaving subordination of individuals under the division of labour, and therewith also the antithesis between mental and physical labour, has vanished . . . after the productive forces have also increased with the all-round development of the individual, and all the springs of cooperative wealth flow more abundantly,

when society can 'inscribe on its banners: from each according to his ability, to each according to his needs'.[30]

But this merely pushes back the inquiry one step further: is the 'communist' stage final, and does history end there? Marx could not of course be expected to provide a blueprint of the future, which would have offended his own scientific principles and detracted from the main task he had set himself in his life. There are, however, occasional glimpses –

When, in the course of development, class distinctions have disappeared, and all production has been concentrated in the hands of a vast association of the whole nation, the public power will lose its political character . . . we shall have an association in which the free development of each is the condition of the free development of all.

The proletariat seizes the state power, and transforms the means of production in the first instance into state property. But in doing this, it puts an end to itself as the proletariat, it puts an end to all class differences and class antagonisms, it puts an end also to the state as the state . . . The government of persons is replaced by the administration of things and the direction of the process of production. The state is not 'abolished', it *withers away*.

The condition of the emancipation of the working class is the abolition of every class, just as the condition of the liberation of the Third Estate, of the bourgeois order, was the abolition of all estates and all (feudal) orders . . . It is only in an order of things in which there are no more classes and class antagonisms that social *evolutions* will cease to be political revolutions.

30. MARX, *Critique of the Gotha Programme* (1875, Eng. edn 1941), p. 14.

Communism is the *positive* abolition of *private property*, of human self-alienation.[31]

We know that when production will be carried on by a 'free association of producers, under their conscious and purposive control', output will be immeasurably greater, so great that 'labour which is determined by need and external purposes ceases'. Then echoing the Saint-Simonians, 'the realm of freedom begins ... that development of human potentiality for its own sake, the true realm of freedom'.[32]

It would be contrary to Marxist philosophy to assume stagnation. The emphasis is on development, as well as on freedom. The next revolution will merely, as all the others before it, settle one cause of struggles in order to create different struggles on a higher plane. Marx knows no heaven in which all is bliss and perfection: the future he sees is one of free growth and further development of the human personality, the epitome of the humanist ideal.

Marx, who consciously placed himself and his analysis 'on the side' of the proletariat, had no difficulty in placing the British political economists as the ideologues of the bourgeoisie. As such, he expected them to become defenders of the *status quo*, transforming current relationships into eternal laws, as soon as the bourgeoisie had fortified its political power after 1689. The same was true of France, even though, because of the difference in the rate of development, some of the ill-effects of the new order were visible earlier, and its benefits felt later than in Britain, so that the critical views of Saint-Simon and Sismondi arose at the same time, or even preceded the apologetics of Bastiat (1801–50) and Say (1767–1832). But in countries such as Germany, the invitation to treat the categories of British capitalist and increasingly

31. *Communist Manifesto* (1930 edn), p. 28; *Anti-Dühring*, pp. 308, 309; *The Poverty of Philosophy*, pp. 146–7; MARX, *Economic and Philosophical Manuscripts* (1844), in T. B. Bottomore, *Karl Marx, Early Writings* (1963), p. 155.

32. *Kapital*, p. 54; Bottomore, p. ix.

laissez-faire society as eternal, inevitably clashed with the experience of the Germans, who were still in the midst of the transition from the feudal order. The needs of 'improving' landlords and mercantilist princes, and the traditional excellence of the training of the bureaucracy, ensured for political economy a widespread attention in the German universities, but the Germans could not be expected to swallow its naïve assumptions. Those, like Friedrich List (1789–1846), who had experience of advanced countries, accepted 'Smithianismus', even though they moderated it to fit it to the needs of Germany. But most of them found it impossible to ignore the evidence of their own recent history and the current experience of much of Central and Eastern Europe, and to grant validity only to the logic of capitalist society, but deny it to all earlier types. On the contrary, being themselves in a position to experience the strains and stresses of passing from one formation of society to another, they were inclined to make the transition and the mechanism behind it the main subject matter of their political economy.

The German historical school of political economists which arose in these conditions thus had much in common with Savigny's historical school of jurisprudence, and with Comtean positivism. According to them, history proceeded in stages, each of which had a recognizable character of its own, determining all facts of society, including its economic relationships, and each, by its own immanent constitution, inevitably prepared the way for and ushered in the next. Their stages were conceived in basic economic terms, savage huntsmen turning into nomadic herdsmen; settled agriculture; towns and industries; commerce and the market economy; and the modern commercial-industrial-agrarian economy. Alternatively, the sequence might be barter-money-credit. Their originality lay not in devising schemes to represent the history of humanity, as an inevitable one-directional ascent of man as a social being, but in exploring in detail both the internal economic, legal, political and social logic of earlier systems, for example feudal society, and the mechanism by which it nurtured in its womb the embryo of the next type of social man who would ultimately destroy it.

As long as bourgeois society still lay in the future, it was possible to be both a good liberal economist and a believer in progress. The so-called 'older school' of historical economists, led by Wilhelm Roscher (1817–94), Bruno Hildebrand (1812–78) and Karl Knies (1821–98) operating in a similar environment, had indeed much in common with the French *philosophes* of the Enlightenment, though formally they were at the opposite pole, propagating a historical, instead of a rationalist, method. As summarized by Knies, in his *Politische Oekonomie vom geschichtlichen Standpunkte* (1853), the view implied that at each stage in the past, the economic system corresponded to the stage of general civilization reached. The present system was no different, being yet another interim stage in the progressive unfolding of historical development, destined to give way, in due course to others –

The 'general laws' of political economy are nothing but an historical explanation and progressive manifestation of the truth. It is only the study of historical development, and the advancement to a recognition of an order and regularity within it, which can allow us to reach a full understanding of the economic position of the present and of the direction in which we are moving.

The changeability of economic laws is not an evil [added Roscher in a work which appeared a year later], but praiseworthy and beneficial, as long as it runs parallel to the changes in nations and their needs. The most varied abstract models need therefore not contradict one another. Each of them may be right, for its nation and its age only; it would be erroneous only if it pretended to be valid for all time.[33]

It has often been urged against the 'School' that they never practised what they preached, and that as soon as they laid aside

33. KNIES, *Politische Oekonomie* (1883 edn, Braunschweig), p. 376; WILHELM ROSCHER, *Die Grundlagen der Nationalökonomie* (1854, Stuttgart, 4 vols., 1858 edn), I, 41.

their methodological preoccupations and wrote about economic matters, they were as eager as their British contemporaries to discover and propagate what looked suspiciously like eternally valid economic 'laws'. On a purely intellectual level, the temptation, particularly for German university professors, of becoming the authors of such 'laws' must have been overwhelming and well-nigh irresistible. The significant fact is surely that despite it, they held the view of the temporary, historicist validity of any 'laws' they might discover.

Within a generation the face of Germany had changed. Inside a Prussian, imperial-militarist social framework, and under a landowning ruling class, the bourgeoisie was riding high after 1870, and the environment had become fully capitalistic. Numerous reforms were still left to fight for, but in the more basic socio-economic sphere, the liberal middle classes had as little wish to change the system fundamentally into some 'higher' stage as had their British counterpart in the eighteenth century. It was possible to hold to the 'historical' view only if one was prepared to visualize another stage, and the 'younger school' of historical economists or 'Socialists of the Chair', men like Gustav Schmoller (1838–1917) or Lujo Brentano (1844–1931) did indeed hold the kind of views which, forty years earlier, had attracted John Stuart Mill to Saint-Simon and Comte. Meanwhile the organized German working class was being won over to Marxism.

Other German economists, however, discovered virtues in the 'classical' political economy which the British and after them the French, had evolved precisely at the same stage of their national economic development. This had not, of course, stood still in the course of the century. In particular, the loss of the dynamic historical element, the vision of social change and progress, and their replacement by 'eternal' laws and categories had made orthodox political economy in the mid-century a hunting ground for unoriginal second-rate practitioners entirely overshadowed by the giants of the Ricardian generation. Around

1870, political economy was transformed into marginalist economics, and with it a key social science became a mathematics, irrefutable as long as it was internally consistent, but utterly lacking in a historical dimension, increasingly divorced from the other social sciences and unable to escape from its assumptions that capitalist categories, values and *mores* are alone and eternally valid. It was a mark of triumph, as of doom, of the new liberal capitalist order.

The important thing was not so much, as Thorold Rogers, an admirer of the German School, put it

that much which popular economists believe to be natural is highly artificial; that what they call laws are often hasty, inconsiderate and inaccurate inductions; and that much which they consider to be demonstrably irrefutable is demonstrably false,[34]

but that by making economics a-historical, the economists made social conservatism orthodox. To advocate further progress by basic social change, as had occurred in the past, was not only politically deplorable, but economically nonsensical.

The ease with which the old science of political economy was destroyed and the new one of marginalist economics accepted in its place would be one of the most astounding features of nineteenth-century intellectual history, were it not that orthodox political economy was by then only an empty shell, and the triumph of the bourgeoisie in Western Europe had made the change inevitable. In Germany, however, the matter was not so easy, since here economic development had been telescoped into so remarkably short a period, that both the preoccupation with the transition from one system to another, and the assumption that the new system was finally valid, were possible. Consequently, Germany plunged into the *Methodenstreit*, of mathematical or abstract-rational versus historical economics. Some of the combatants, notably Carl Menger, were well aware of what

34. *The Economic Interpretation of History* (1888, 7th edn 1909), pp. vi–vii.

was at stake, since for him economics had as its business the giving of advice how to improve the present state, not how to abolish it.

Their loyalty to the existing order did not mean that economists were necessarily pessimistic about the future. The Great Depression led to some doubts, and helped the spread of the marginalist doctrines which did not depend on social progress. Others, like Francis Galton, doubted man's ability to control an increasingly complex society. But, on the whole, economists, entrepreneurs and city men were optimistic: they had found the key to rising wealth, and with it, to social peace and respectability. 'Progress' meant that the framework could remain as it was, Britain would be ever more efficient in supplying the world with manufactures, everyone would be better off, and the working classes would become increasingly like the middle classes in behaviour and outlook – except that they would go on being content to work for mere wages.

Meanwhile, however, the blow of the Darwinian theory had fallen. Charles Darwin (1809–82), who was to dominate the century after him in his own field as much as Marx dominated his, derived his notion of the mechanism of natural selection from Malthus' morose description of capitalist society. This is not to say that it is thereby suspect: its simultaneous development by Alfred Russell Wallace (1823–1913), and its victory over all the combined forces of Christian obscurantism in Victorian Britain, prove the aptness of the theory for the then state of knowledge. It does mean that it was exceptionally easy to translate the concepts of biological evolution into social terms and apply them to the study of society. Darwin had vastly lengthened the time span within which social evolution could be presumed to have taken place; he had made continuous, inevitable, (and basically, purposeless) evolution of social organisms much more acceptable by analogy with biological evolution and made the opposite, a static view of the world, impossible to hold by anyone aspiring to a scientific outlook.

The acceptance of Darwinism in the social sciences was not nearly as complete as among biologists. But it set the fashion, and became, for a time, a kind of model, just as Newton's physics had been, nearly two centuries earlier.

The impact on anthropology and ethnography, then advancing in great strides from their infancy, was the most immediate, and a scientific evolutionary scheme was quickly taken for granted. Thus E. B. Tylor had no doubt that

the conditions of culture among the various societies of mankind, in so far as it is capable of being investigated on general principles, is a subject apt for the study of laws of human thought and action. On the one hand the uniformity which so largely pervades civilization may be ascribed in great measure, to the uniform action of uniform causes; while on the other its various grades may be regarded as stages of development or evolution, each the outcome of previous history and about to do its proper part in shaping the history of the future.[35]

The most influential adaptation of Darwinism to the social sciences, however, was that of Herbert Spencer (1820–1903).

Even before the publication of Darwin's *Origin of Species*, he had argued that progress did not consist in greater wealth, greater knowledge, or a higher moral state: these were but symptoms. Its real nature was the change in the internal structure of society, which is expressed by an ever widening division of labour, itself a natural phenomenon –

It is not by the 'hero as king', any more than by 'collective wisdom', that men have been segregated into producers, wholesale distributors and retail distributors.

Few writers have been as contemptuous of the role of the individual in history, and as convinced of the inevitability of its course: the ruler

may disturb, he may retard, or he may aid the natural process of organization; but the general *course* of this process is beyond his

35. *Primitive Culture* (1871), p. 1.

control. Nay, more than this is true. Those who regard the histories of societies as the histories of their great men, and think that these great men shape the fate of their societies, overlook the truth that such great men are the products of their societies ... Society is a growth and not a manufacture.[36]

Darwin and Huxley had opened up the possibility of integrating man more closely in the natural universe, making him less subject to special treatment, and thereby making it easier to apply science to society and to history. Spencer had found them particularly congenial, for he had assimilated his sociology, as Darwin had his biology, to the experience of mid-Victorian capitalism, the greatest, and perhaps, the last period of competitive and unplanned growth. The impersonal powers of history were like 'the market' under competition, operating as an aggregation of innumerable and divergent wills, rather than by the plan of a single will.

Spencer, like Comte, believes that the universe is subject to laws, including social laws, and that it is the fate of mankind, in its national societies, to pass through a series of cultural stages. Both equate evolution and progress. But on the question of the ultimate aim and direction, they are at opposite poles. In place of Comte's superior intelligence, using the state power to organize society, Spencer sees the next stage as the total abolition of Government, and the maintenance of social cohesion by feeling, to which the intellect will serve as a guide only –

Practically, the popular character and the social state determines what ideas shall be current; instead of the current ideas determining the social state and the character.[37]

In place of Comte's organized humanity, Spencer hopes for individuation, for anarchist individualism.

36. *Essays: Scientific, Political and Speculative* (3 vols., 1868–78), I, 385, 387–8; also Essay I, 'Progress, its Law and Cause'.
37. 'Of the Classification of the Sciences', pp. 37–8 (quoted in MILL, *Auguste Comte*, 1891, pp. 102–3); also SPENCER, 'Reasons for Dissenting from the Philosophy of M. Comte', *Essays*, III, 69–70.

Darwin's biology confirmed Spencer's early optimism on the future of society. The 'survival of the fittest' postulated ever better adaptation, which, in human terms, meant social adaptation and improvement. He never firmly decided whether this would come about unthinkingly, or whether men were expected to bring it about by self-restraint and collaboration; in other words, Spencer never quite solved the dilemma between the Lamarckian and Darwinian views. But he could see that the technical area of control consisted of ever larger units, within which there was therefore an ever larger area of internal peace and industry, developing in almost Saint-Simonian terms 'industrial' out of the 'militarist' society, as one of the most striking examples of improvement arising out of the ubiquitous principle of differentiation.

Since he believed that 'human well-being is in accordance with the Divine will', and the 'ultimate purpose of creation [is] the production of the greatest amount of happiness', Spencer had no difficulty in postulating, for the first time clearly since Condorcet, the biological improvement of man, so that 'the ultimate development of the ideal man is logically certain ... the things we call our immorality [must] disappear ... man must become perfect'.[38] The ideal seems individual, but it has been possible for socialists to accept Darwinism on the grounds that the socialist *society* will be the 'fittest' to survive. Other Darwinians, like D. G. Ritchie, could argue that while the early stages of evolution were instinctive, the later ones are conscious and deliberate, and therefore they could allow for social control.

While Spencer's social Darwinism had some intellectual content, for others the temptation to see in British economic and imperial power the proof of being the 'fittest', was too great to be resisted. One of the best examples of Victorian middle-class smugness in this field was *Physics and Politics, or Thoughts on the Application of the Principles of 'Natural Selection' and 'Inheritance' to Political Society* (1872) by Walter Bagehot

38. *Social Statics* (1850, 2nd edn 1868), pp. 81, 448, 79, 80.

(1826–77). It begins promisingly: 'One peculiarity of this age is the sudden acquisition of much physical knowledge', and makes the point early on, that the idea of progress is not only very recent, but still purely Western –

Only a few nations, and those of European origin, advance; and yet these think … such advance to be inevitable, natural and eternal.

Building on a simple-minded view of politics which completely ignores economic or social developments, the author's laws of human progress seems to be that the strongest nations always prevail, 'and in certain marked peculiarities the strongest tend to be the best', in each type of society the 'most attractive', or 'best', character tends to prevail, and 'natural selection' within human society operates by way of competition. However, since it was the objective of the book to discover the political requisites of progress, or how to help the 'old Eastern and customary civilizations' to become like the 'new Western and changeable civilizations', Bagehot's advice is that it is ideas that make history, so that our task is 'to pour what we can of a civilization whose spirit is progress into the form of a civilization whose spirit is fixity'.[39]

Even if Bagehot's work ignored virtually all the achievements of historical and sociological inquiries of the preceding hundred years, and offered the most shallow truisms with an air of scientific discovery, it is yet worth recalling for two reasons. First, it illustrates the almost total acceptance of the idea of progress in Victorian Britain and the West, but in terms which imply that the glory of humanity can scarcely go farther. But secondly, it was one of the first to include in the idea of progress also the notion that the rest of the world should experience it independently, and not merely as a colonial backyard of Europe.

Much of the contemporary literature was even shallower than Bagehot, a sad decline from the Enlightenment attempts of

39. ibid., pp. 1, 42, 43, 81, 156, 157.

evolving a theory of the development of human society. Historians lost interest, like political economists, and for much the same reason. Perhaps the most striking exception was T. H. Buckle (1821–62), whose *Introduction to the History of Civilization in England* (1857, 1861), was planned on a vast scale, but left unfinished because of his tragic early death.

Buckle's ideas developed directly out of the Enlightenment, and Cartesian and Newtonian science. The scientific search for laws and regularities should be extended to history and to the human intellect, for man's action in history depends on motives, and the motives on antecedents, so that if we knew the latter, we could predict the former. Already much that had once appeared random and inexplicable could now be shown to be subject to laws, particularly, as Comte and Mill had already observed, the statistical laws of large numbers. 'The whole scope and tendency of modern thought force upon our mind conceptions of regularity and of law.'[40] Unlike his religious adversaries, who believed that the deity had so bungled the creation of the world that it had to be corrected by miracles later, Buckle's universe was created in a perfect state from the beginning, and has obeyed its laws, including the 'laws of mankind', ever since.

In Buckle's determinist history there are two main influences. One is the physical, material environment, particularly in the earlier civilizations. The other, increasingly important in the higher stages of society, and forming an inner immanent, rather than an external determinant, was intellectual development. This clearly did not derive from greater capacity of the human intellect, but from its greater social opportunity. Buckle could not conceive of a determinant of history other than ideas, and there the choice lay between morals and intellect. But while moral insights had not changed in the past three millennia, knowledge had advanced enormously, and both civilization and morals had been raised by it and with it. It is the scientific discoveries which

40. *Civilization in England* (1904 edn), p. 901.

survive the shock of empires, outlive the struggles of rival creeds, and witness the decay of successive religions.

The intellectual principle has an activity and a capacity for adaptation, which ... is quite sufficient to account for the extraordinary progress that, during several centuries, Europe has continued to make.[41]

Since Buckle offended the religious susceptibilities and the clerical opinion which still dominated academic history teaching in Britain, he was persistently misrepresented by the critics in his lifetime. His laws and generalizations were not meant to predict individual events, but general social processes. It was his merit to have included the whole of society in his history, supported by his immense erudition, and to have demanded the use of 'laws' discovered in economics, psychology, and other social sciences, by historians, even if he saw the mainspring of progress in the advance of the intellect and of science. He thought the *laissez faire* which he admired in the present, to be representative of the spirit of the age which would at last assure untrammelled progress in the future.

Buckle published just in advance of Darwin, and therefore missed some of the stimulus of the idea of biological evolution, but the concepts of evolution and of progress, even without Darwin, were very much in the air. J. W. Draper (1811–82), for example, writing at the same time, boldly stated the object of the book to be to demonstrate that

social advancement is as completely under the control of natural law as is bodily growth. The life of an individual is a miniature of the life of a nation.

Within this physiological model

the procession of nations in time ... is ... a predetermined, a solemn march, in which all must join, ever moving, ever restlessly advancing, encountering and enduring an inevitable succession of events.

There are differences in the experiences of nations, just as

41. ibid., p. 104.

there are between individuals, and accidents may befall them so that they die prematurely: but physiologically, they have the same basic stages of birth, growth, ageing and death prescribed for them. 'For everyone there is an orderly way of progress to its final term, whatever that term might be.' All societies have to pass (in a curious mixture of positivism and medicine) through the Age of Credulity, the Age of Inquiry, the Age of Faith, the Age of Reason and the Age of Decrepitude. These can be found, not only in Europe or Asia, but very similarly, in the isolated States of pre-Columbian America. In order to survive, institutions have to change in the right direction of advance. In a world of immutable laws, for Draper, as for Kant and Buckle, historical determinism depends on distance. Close to, all appears chaotic; from a cosmic viewpoint, there is no free will at all.

The progress of societies, like that of human children, is from the reflexive, to the instinctive, and ultimately the intellectual, when it is 'always advancing'. So almost word for word like Buckle, Draper asserts that

historically ... we find that the intellectual has always led the way in social advancement, the moral having been subordinated thereto. The former has been the mainspring of the movement, the latter passively affected.[42]

The future lies with intellectual improvements, better education, and a greater understanding of social laws, to guide our actions to fit in with the demands of historical science.

This human physiological metaphor, which after all must assume death and decay also, and the economists' conviction that no higher form of society was possible, might have been expected to curb the expectation of further progress. But the Victorian world was too optimistic for this. It is often forgotten that there were two springs of optimism hidden in it, reinforcing each other, yet quite distinct, and destined soon to

42. *A History of the Intellectual Development of Europe* (1863, London edn 1875, 2 vols.), I, iii, II, 393, 360.

take different courses. One was the bourgeois optimism of the economists, the leader writers and the politicians, that their society had at last found the key to material improvement, and that the whole of Europe was following admiringly in their wake. The other was the proletarian optimism, going back to the Saint-Simonians and to Marx, that society was inevitably heading for a drastic change, in which the oppressed would at last come into their own, and the basis for real progress would be laid. And some, like the trade-union leaders of the British working classes, and socialist intellectuals everywhere, even enjoyed the luxury of holding both simultaneously.

Behind both lay the undeniable material growth in the West, and its political ascendancy, its imperial or gunboat domination, coupled with its total economic control over the rest of the world. The Great Exhibition of 1851, in particular, had done much to convert a wide public from the idea of 'improvement' to the idea of 'progress'. And when, from the middle of the nineteenth century on, it became possible in Britain and the U.S.A., and soon elsewhere also, to make some of the products and benefits of the new system of production available to the great mass of the producing classes, both opposing schools of thought felt this to be a confirmation of their ideas of progress: for the bourgeois, a confirmation that what was good for him, could at last be shown to be good for the country as a whole; for the proletarian, his first small victory, the first step upon an advance which would ultimately usher in his chapter in the story of the upward march of man.

Among the economists the path led from the 'scientific' statistical proofs of Leone Levi or Robert Giffen, to the more thoughtful, measured reflections of Marshall (1842–1924) –

The hope [he says at the beginning of his work], that poverty and ignorance may gradually be extinguished, derives much support from the steady progress of the working classes during the nineteenth century ... Some [artisans] already lead a more refined and noble life than did the majority of the upper classes even a century ago.

And the last chapter derides the pessimists, the believers in the 'romantic exaggerations of the happiness of past ages', and the doubters in the 'method of progress, the work of which if slow is yet solid'.[43]

The historians, dominated by the Whig school and little concerned with the fate of the working classes, were even more certain than Voltaire had been, that the history of the world was one long prelude to the glories of their own age. Macaulay (1800–59), believed that his society was 'the most enlightened generation of the most enlightened people that ever existed'. Acton (1834–1902) at the end of the century, was no less certain of progress; and Mendell Creighton's introduction to the *Cambridge Modern History* asserted magisterially at the outset of a work that was intended to set a seal to a generation of historical scholarship –

we are bound to assume, as the scientific hypothesis on which history has been written, a progress in human affairs.[44]

Even Sir Henry Maine (1822–88), whose instincts were totally conservative, saw history as an evolution to the perfection of his own society, and similar unquestioning views could be quoted from the French, the Americans and the Germans by the end of the century. It was strongest among those, like H. G. Wells (1866–1946), who had some inkling of the power of science.

In the purely abstract sphere, the sphere of the development of ideas, there is a clear line of progression, ever since the rise of modern science in the sixteenth century, from the belief in the inevitability of the advancement of scientific knowledge and the scientific method to that of advancement in human and social affairs. The consequent assurance of the inevitability of progress seemed confirmed beyond dispute by the successes of the application of science to industry in the eighteenth and nineteenth cen-

43. *Principles of Economics* (1890, 8th edn 1946), pp. 3, 4, 722.
44. ACTON, *A Lecture on the Study of History* (1895); *Cambridge Modern History*, I, (Cambridge, 1902), p. 4.

turies. But this intellectually acceptable doctrine would not have found any widespread support, had it not been confirmed by the experience of at least one class, the bourgeoisie. These were the centuries of its triumph. It rose to power at home, grasped its historic opportunity of vastly increasing man's and society's power over nature, and, based on a small corner of Europe, made itself master of a world which was now larger and more accessible than ever before. Against this experience, any doubts about the uncertainty of progress lingering from the memory of earlier centuries or other continents, were bound to vanish –

Synthesizing the history of values, it is correct to say that from Francis Bacon to Pasteur, from Jean Bodin to Spencer, from Campanella to Herder, from Descartes to Comte and Berthelot, the vast current has an incontestable unity which corresponds to the rise and maturity of the bourgeoisie in the west.[45]

The nineteenth century was the bourgeois century. Its own progress in power, wealth and culture was plain for all to see. The idea of progress not only fitted its own history best, it also proved a useful instrument with which to stifle the anguished protests of those who suffered, and to weaken the determination of the class that armed itself to supplant its rule. Though there were some doubts, and many signs that all was not well for the future, they could safely be ignored until the explosion of 1914.

45. GEORGES FRIEDMANN, *La Crise du Progrès. Esquisse d'histoire des idées 1895–1935,* (Paris, 2nd edn 1936), p. 10.

CHAPTER FOUR

A DIGRESSION:
DOUBTERS AND PESSIMISTS

UNDERLYING the idea of progress, and indeed any idea which attempts to probe into the future, is the conviction that there are, at least, some historical 'laws' or valid generalizations which link the events of the past and allow some form of prediction – or, in other words, that history is in some respects a science similar to other sciences. This assumption has been widely disputed, and it is necessary to devote some pages to a discussion of some of the objections raised and to the answers supplied by those who believe in progress. The remainder of the chapter will discuss views which, while agreeing that historical analysis and synthesis are possible, have used them to show that mankind is not heading for progress in any accepted sense.

It should be stressed at the outset that the ideas of nihilism or despair, if held by a significant number of people, are just as likely to derive from their social experience as are the optimistic ideas of progress. Widespread pessimism began to appear in the West only towards the end of the nineteenth century, when it became clear that the social problem had not been solved and there was no sign of a solution; when the leading bourgeois nations, having divided the world among themselves, began to feel claustrophobic and turn inward on each other; and when a particular phase of history appeared to have run its course. The clashes, the destruction, and the failures of the years 1914–45, a virtually continuous period of wars and depressions, were as traumatic for the West as the years 1789–1815 had been for those nurtured on the Enlightenment, and only towards the end, did the need to defend what values the West possessed against the new European barbarism rekindle some of the earlier hope and self-confidence. Not all succumbed to the more fashionable doubts, doubts not only about progress but about the possibility of foretelling it; indeed, they were never more than a minority opinion. Some looked upon the growing powers of production, the growing flow of consumer goods and predicted, correctly as it turned out, that there was life in the old dog yet, and a future for liberal capitalist society. Others, more significantly perhaps, invented false or 'perverse' progress, alleging, for example, that there were no longer owners and proletarians, but managers and employees only, and that there were still many such progresssive transformations to come under 'welfare capitalism' – a characteristic reaction of a class that fears for its future. But the idealistic nihilism of Croce (1866–1952), Ortega y Gasset (1883–1955) or Collingwood, (1889–1943), or the hostility towards a scientific history of Rickert (1863–1936), Dilthey (1833–1911) or Meinecke (1862–1954), in his younger years, were not purely intellectual phenomena, but closely reflected the spirit, and the social realities, of their age.

The debate on whether history is a science and its relationship to other sciences would fill a small library. Some of the issues have become extremely complex, and it would clearly go much beyond the scope of this volume to trace them even in outline. A few hints must suffice, and with them, an indication of the minimal beliefs found necessary by those who held to progress and with whom this book is concerned.

One aspect of the nature of the attack may be learnt from the extreme position represented by Rickert and developed in the 1890s as a reaction to the optimism that wanted to make history simply into a positivist science. According to Rickert, a clear dividing line exists between the natural sciences, which are 'nomothetic', concerned with and able to develop abstract general laws, and the 'cultural sciences', including history, which are 'ideographic', and are concerned with the unique, the non-recurrrent. Historians might, Croce would agree, use their knowledge of other, real sciences, as a painter might use some knowledge of chemistry, but by itself, it was an art, and its essence was that it was composed of unique events. Again, man himself, like humanity as a whole, was constantly learning, growing and changing –

Man, in a word, has no nature; what he has is . . . history.[1]

A further, and related, view hostile to any certainty about progress is that no objective view of history is really possible. One could hold with the historicism of Meinecke (in all but his last years), or its more developed form in Mannheim's 'sociology of knowledge', that each age, each person, perhaps, would have a different view of an event, would pick on different aspects as important, and would judge differently, and all might be equally valid, and this would clearly make any 'scientific' generalizations impossible. Hayek put it in the form that the natural sciences are 'objective', while the social ones are 'subjective', and even their facts have no meaning unless put in a historically and socially conditioned unique form, and von Mises similarly speaks of a 'methodological dualism' between nature and human thought and action. A variant, introducing even more mysticism, was developed by Collingwood, who thought that true history could not deal in 'causes', because it was concerned only with the thoughts of the actors of an event, which are

the inside of the event itself . . . All history is the history of thought,

rather than the less meaningful 'outside' of events.[2] Dilthey, who had great influence in Germany, similarly believed that physical objects are to us mere appearances, while minds are 'real realities', so that the historians' insight and understanding into mental processes, the 'higher understanding', was the significant one. But as psychology thus became central to his historical explanation, some science was introduced by the back door.

A third objection relates less to the nature of the historian

1. ORTEGA Y GASSET, 'History as a system', in Klibanski and Paton, *Philosophy and History* (Oxford, 1936), p. 313.
2. COLLINGWOOD, *The Idea of History* (Oxford, 1946), p. 215.

than to the facts of history. Even if regularities and 'laws' existed in some social situations, history is often determined by the accidents of personalities. If Napoleon had died of an infantile disease, or Lenin been killed in a train crash before October 1917, the whole of the history of their period would have looked different, and the accidents of their survival (or, perhaps, of the deaths of other potential, but unknown leaders) cannot possibly be encompassed within any historically 'explanatory' theory. The Great Man, or accident, view of history is also linked with the issue of free will and determinisn. For if the course of history is determined by some general forces, these must also determine the actions of each of the individuals in the society in question, and therefore free will, decision making, and moral responsibilities are illusions, and man cannot make, or influence, his own history.

Finally, it has often been pointed out that most, or all, the predictions made on the basis of historical generalizations have turned out to be wrong. This does not necessarily preclude the possibility of a more nearly correct theory in the future, or of such a theory in principle, but it clearly weakens the case for one.

The answer to these objections have been many and varied. Several have been touched upon incidentally in earlier chapters. Here we shall limit ourselves to outlining the minimum which men have to believe in order to sustain confidence in progress.

In recent years the belief in the total reliability of a predictive social science has been much less comprehensive than in the days of Saint-Simon and Comte. Above all, it is recognized that the validity of social-historical 'laws' depends much on the scope of the inquiry, and on the kind of questions asked, rather than on philosophic certainties established outside the context of historical studies.

On the question of free will and the role of the individual, for example, it had been accepted since Kant's well-known formulation that what appears random or capricious if seen singly, is a

steady and continuous, though slow, development of certain great
predispositions in our nature;

or in Hume's words, that

what depends upon few persons is, in a great measure, to be ascribed
to chance, or secret and unknown causes; what arises from a great
number may often be accounted for by determinate and known
causes.[3]

Since then, the idea has been expressed repeatedly by historians
ranging from Engels to Buckle.

The difference between unit and aggregate, between predictability at the level of individual biography, and at the level of
society (at which the generalizations discussed in this book are
made), must form the most elementary base of historical understanding. Just, as one suspects, no student could advance far in
the study of physics who failed to see the difference between the
unpredictability of a single atom and the regularities of a mass of
them, and the relationship between them; and no student could
go far in economics without understanding the differences between the roles of a single buyer and seller, and the market as a
whole, in a competitive situation, and the relationship between
them. The crucial relationship between individual freedom of
action and historical determinism ought to form a *sine qua non*
of historical understanding. Yet among historians and philosophers of history, the inability to see that both freedom of choice
and determinism are, and must be, simultaneously true, depending on the level of generalization, is found not only among raw
beginners, but even among those eminent enough to be found in
print. And if it is true that

the central assumption of the individualist position . . . is that no
social tendency exists which could not be altered *if* the individuals

3. KANT, *Idea of a Universal History*, pp. 418–19; HUME, 'Rise and
Progress of Arts and Sciences', in *Essays, Moral, Political and Literary*
(1903 edn), p. 112.

concerned both wanted to alter it and possess the appropriate information,[4]

then it is clear the 'individualist position' has failed to grasp even the most elementary mechanism of history. It is, of course, at the level of society as a whole, or even of mankind as a whole, that assumptions of continuous progress have been made, and the preoccupation with whole social systems, and with universal history, is a marked feature of all theories of progress.

Many historians would go beyond the minimal position sketched here, and would say that men, influential, leading and 'great' men in particular, do not act or choose at random. The choices open to them are necessarily given by the framework of society: no one in England today can choose to be a slaveholder. But even among the choices open, the general direction of options taken is, or could be, predictable in a given dynamic situation. Above all, leaders can lead in a certain direction only because their followers are ready for them. As Tolstoy expressed it, many commands may be given, but history is determined by those which are actually obeyed.

Little time need be spent on the remaining suggestion that the declaration of the inevitability of some tendency will paralyse the will, and lead to fatalism. In practice, the opposite is usually true, and the most determined actors in history are those who are certain that they are on the side of the inevitable. Indeed, the growing self-consciousness and understanding of social and historical action is one of the observed facts which has been taken into account by most prophets of progress from the mid-eighteenth century onwards. In sum –

such theories as those of Comte and Marx are theories about what men do, about how they behave; they are not theories about what happens to men no matter what they do.[5]

4. J. W. N. WATKINS, 'Historical Explanation in the Social Sciences', reprinted in Gardiner, *Theories of History* (Glencoe, Ill., 1959), p. 506.
5. JOHN PLAMENATZ, *Man and Society* (2 vols., 1963 edn), II, 425.

The second main issue, how far history is a science for which generalizations with certain predictive powers are valid, is more complex. The more recent tendency has been to avoid looking for the absolute certainty of Newtonian laws, and to define more clearly the limits within which 'laws', 'tendencies' and predictions might operate. Even Turgot had been less than total in his determinism when he stated that –

History in the eyes of a philosopher [had] to unveil the influence of general and necessary causes, along with that of particular causes, and that of the free action of great men.

Further, today even the physical sciences are less concerned with certainties than with probabilities, uncertainties and the historical context, and are therefore much nearer to the historian's position –

Historians can explain some events and states in just the sense in which natural scientists explain such events and ... their explanations of such events and states must and can be defined by an appeal to experience.

Simultaneously, the formulations of modern historians are looser, and their work has been correctly described by Hempel as 'explanation sketches', or as 'pragmatic' rather than 'predictive' laws, which recall the 'empirical laws' definition of John Stuart Mill –

Historical hypotheses are not general or universal propositions. They cannot be falsified by a single exception. Testing them largely means trying to discover the boundaries of the area within which they seem reasonably valid.[6]

6. TURGOT, *Notes on Universal History* (1750), in W. W. Stephens, *Life and Writings of Turgot*, p. 175; MORTON WHITE, *Foundations of Historical Knowledge* (New York, 1965), p. 218; C. G. HEMPEL, 'The Foundation of General Laws in History', *J. of Philosophy* (1942), reprinted in Gardiner, pp. 334 *et seq.*, together with much of the debate it engendered; GERSCHENKRON, *Economic Backwardness in Historical Perspective* (Cambridge, Mass., 1962), p. 360.

The looseness of these modern definitions has allowed us to see to what extent apparently opposing theories differed merely by the range of conditions they took for granted. Thus all historians take it for granted that man is mortal, but not quite all take the geographic environment for granted, and those who do not, like Montesquieu or Ferguson, appear to have this as their distinguishing mark of their theory. Again, before Marx, most historians took the economic system with its laws for granted and discussed political leadership; Marx, on the other hand, took for granted that each group of men acting in history will throw up an appropriate leadership, but examined the relations of production in detail. Others, again, very similarly, made social psychology the centre of their theories. This may be summarized by the statement that historical 'explanation' is a picking out of the 'abnormal', the 'difference-maker', or the cause of which the listener is ignorant or which he has in the past been prone to underrate, and this may represent all of Mill's gap between 'the cause' and 'the whole cause'. These differences in emphasis usually reflect fundamental differences as to what constitutes the mainspring, the basic mechanism of historical change; but these are sometimes smaller than appears at first sight, and still allow all concerned to agree on the general proposition of future progress.

All, however, agree that some law and some generalization there must be. A unique event would be indescribable –

If we push the doctrine of the unique individual and the unique episode too far, we only end by making it impossible to reflect on the past ... The past could not be narrated as a story of chances and changes; and indeed it would not even be a story, for between a succession of absolutely unique particles there can be no thread that would hold a narrative together. The study of history could only be a burden to the memory, and would lose most of its educational point.[7]

Isaiah Berlin (b. 1909) once suggested that the majority of

7. HERBERT BUTTERFIELD, *Man on His Past*, p. 102.

human beings, including even historians, do not behave as if they believed in determinism, that is a 'fixed pattern', because they pass judgement on other men's actions. This appeal to practical common sense and experience is interesting for two reasons. First, for the naïve fallacy, noted above, of confusing the laws governing society and the choices open to individuals. But secondly, if issues of historical understanding are really to be settled by such arguments, then the evidence is clearly the other way, for ordinary persons, including historians outside their studies, do act as if they took social laws, regularities and the predictability of the actions of other members of society for granted. In real life, what would the anti-determinist historian do? We can see him sallying forth every morning, furtively clutching his revolver, for there is no assurance that the police are still on duty, or that his neighbours have not formed armed gangs to rob and murder all passers-by. He walks everywhere, for he cannot rely on the workers at the power station or the bus depot to have turned up to work. And his briefcase is bulging with goods for barter, for the banks might impound his deposits, or people might refuse pound notes as being valueless; indeed, there is no certainty even that anyone would want to barter away good, nourishing food or clothing for the very inferior historical philosophy which is all he has to offer in return.

The fantasy is not entirely nonsensical. History can show actual examples for each of the diversions from the normal feared by our paranoid philosopher; and each of the neighbours, workers, bank managers, etc. is 'free' to produce just those results, in J. W. N. Watkins' sense quoted above, if all of them 'wanted' to produce them. But of course, the work of the world, especially in a complex capitalist society, would come to a complete halt, if we asssumed 'free will', rather than regular behaviour, in the mass. Instead, we let the police deal with individual deviations; and we attempt to form social laws to predict and 'understand' such behaviour as strikes, sabotage, or runaway inflation.

Any form of historical determinism is largely based on the 'laws' and generalizations of other sciences. Some, like the assurance that all men must die, derive from the biological sciences; but these tend to be taken for granted by historians, since, as in all fields of human knowledge, this is the only method of avoiding turning every question into an issue of the total universe and total experience. The 'laws' over which historians dispute are generally laws of other social sciences. It has therefore been clear, since the days of Saint-Simon and Comte, that the closest links exist between history and the other sciences of society, and one cannot but feel that occasionally historians would save themselves much hard work and thought if they had an inkling of the work of the sociologists – and vice versa. For in the end, the differences are largely a matter of degree and of drawing boundaries.

History cannot be entirely without laws, generalizations, and consequent attempts to predict the future (or, indeed, the unknown past), nor are other social sciences entirely without interest in the unique. Each science has elements of both, but history is at one end of the spectrum, the end which is most concerned with the unique sequence of events, and least with their regularities. But there would be no subject of study, without the regularities assumed as given, against which the actual historical story is seen as being acted out. The relationship has something in it of the relationship between geology and physics, or medicine and biology, or most closely the medical observation of a single person against the background of medical science. Any diagnosis or treatment, both of which have elements of prediction, must be centred on the individual in question, but would be of little value without the science of medicine in general. So it is with history and the laws of social science. The invention of the steam-engine condenser by Watt was a unique event, but it would be a poor history that did not see it against the background of other inventions, or contemporary demands for power, or the role of technology in industrial revolutions. This

is all that is required to sustain a belief in progress; and it is difficult to see how any meaningful history could be conceived without it.

The insistence on the significance of the laws of other social
sciences as one element in human progress in the modern world
has, however, invited an attack from the opposite direction, particularly from those trained in the thought processes of economics. They agree with a limited degree of determinism; they
admit the possibility of valid social laws, within their usual
limitations; and they allow the distinction between individual
and social behaviour. Indeed, their science is based on the
assumption that actual social developments are the unintended
results of the multifariously motivated actions of innumerable
individuals. To that extent, Hayek (b. 1899) is very much in the
tradition of Ferguson, Smith, Marx and the Darwinians in his
belief that

social studies . . . are concerned with men's actions, and their aim
is to explain the unintended and undesigned results of the actions
of many men.

But from this base is derived the conviction that human understanding and human action are legitimate only in small-scale
partial planning and control, where idea can clash with idea, and
interest with interest. Once we attempt to understand, and to
control the whole of society, and presume to 'holism' or to 'Utopian engineering' to take the place of Smith's 'invisible hand',
our inevitable ignorance will lead us not only to do immediate
damage, but also to kill off that freedom and spontaneity which
alone can guarantee progress and make it worth while. Thus
Karl Popper (b. 1902) holds that our social science is at best
capable of 'piecemeal social engineering', that is the possible improvement of limited areas of society, where the damage would
be minimal, and there would be a constant and impartial reference to the rest of society to judge the correctness and value of

the plan offered. The benefit of the social sciences is that they can show us what we cannot do.[8]

This doctrine turns largely on our ignorance, and assumes that it is legitimate to tackle the large unit, in this case society, as a whole, only after the small unit has been mastered. But it does not follow in the least that knowledge always proceeds from the small to the large, or from the factor to the product. The issue had some vogue, and was much debated in the days of Comte, Mill and Spencer, and no such law of progress of knowledge could then be established; today, in the age of nuclear physics, it would surely be impossible to hold any longer to the view that the respectable, 'normal' scientific path is to tackle the unit component before manipulating the complex aggregate. Man makes progress in knowledge and uses it to shape his environment, where he can and where he needs to. A large body, like a society, contains more 'facts', and is therefore more difficult to 'know' fully than one of its components, say the behaviour of rival boards of directors of joint-stock companies, but it might also be more subject to regularities or affected by fewer significant influences.

The attraction of this type of objection cannot be gainsaid. To those of us brought up in the West it conjures up the golden age of liberalism, particularly in Britain and the U.S.A., where capitalist society was at its most promising and progressive, in an environment of free competition among comparable units, without restraint, privilege or central planning. It is no accident that nostalgia for this age should be so strong in Central Europe, where the inevitably uneven development of European capitalism led to the emergence of finance capital, monopolistic industry and central Government control almost as soon as mercantilist restrictionism had been destroyed, thus cheating the

8. HAYEK, *The Counter-Revolution of Science* (Glencoe, Ill., 1952), p. 25; POPPER, *The Poverty of Historicism* (1944–5; paperback edn 1961), pp. 64, 70; and 'Prediction and Prophecy in the Social Sciences', in GARDINER, pp. 279–82.

population of that glorious interlude of freedom in which much of what is best in Western liberalism was born.

But the clock cannot be turned back, and the society sighed for by Hayek, Mises and Popper cannot be reconstituted. Today's economy consists of units of a size which makes society-wide planning of their actions inevitable; and society is so complex that no Government can leave the state of employment, or the foreign balance of payments, entirely to market forces. In any case, as Galbraith has emphasized, 'the market' is no longer wholly the master of the individual supplier, but is subject to his influence, just as a trade union can help to determine the wage level, and perhaps even the productivity on which it is based. Some social control is inevitable, ubiquitous, and extending; and acknowledged or not, it implies a set of predictions, based on a reading of history and on social laws.

One final underlying objection to the belief in a rational history must be examined, and it is one which is particularly destructive of any doctrine of progress. This may grant that there are inner necessities which drive all societies onwards and upwards; but, it would point to the numerous historical examples of just such progressive societies being overwhelmed by a power from outside, a barbarian invasion perhaps, itself no doubt also the outcome of some inner inevitable development, yet leading to the destruction of a superior civilization by an inferior one. In Meinecke's words, it is

a gateway through which something senseless constantly threatens to break into history and often enough has broken into it.[9]

For this there can be no social laws of development, no regularities, and no predictions. Yet it is precisely such irruptions which have brought human progress to a halt in the past, and emphasized the uniqueness of the unrolling of the fate of humanity in time.

9. *Aphorism- and Skizzen*, quoted by W. STARK, Introduction to Meinecke's *Machiavellism* (1924, Engl. edn 1957), p. XXXV.

It might be noted that this is a reservation, rather than an outright rejection of the main thesis. If a medical check-up which came to the conclusion that an individual was healthy and had a good few decades to live yet, were followed by an accident in which the individual was run over by a bus and killed on the same day, we would not thereby be led to deny the scientific character of the medical investigation. On the other hand, if fatal accidents began to follow regularly on check-ups, we might have to take them into account. Not all invasions are as unexpected and inexplicable in terms of the society's own development as the appearance of the Spaniards in the land of the Inca. The rise of the power of the Barbarians along the frontiers of the Roman Empire, or of the Arabs who threatened Medieval Europe, were not without their link with the social development of the society under attack.

Yet there is some force in the reservation, and nearly all theoreticians of progress have felt obliged to deal with it. The answer they gave was almost universally the same. The fatal accidents which befell civilizations from without were much more numerous in the past, when the civilizations themselves were not very advanced and had not risen much above those of the barbarians. But in recent centuries the European West has pulled so far ahead, has put up a civilization so much higher than that of still backward outsiders, and has so fully opened up the whole of the rest of the world, as to make unpleasant surprises less and less likely and ultimately unthinkable. It was precisely this success of the bourgeois, capitalist West in this respect which helped to nourish and fortify the early doctrines of progress. This assurance was well expressed by Condorcet, summarizing the optimism of his century –

There is only one event, a new invasion of Asia by the Tartars, that could prevent this revolution, and ... this event is now impossible.[10]

10. *Sketch*, p. 178.

We must now turn to another line of thought which, in sad decline from Condorcet's invincible optimism, believed that there was a sense in history, but that it pointed to a fall rather than a rise. This *malaise* also is a sign that members of a powerful class are beginning to sense the doom of their historic role, and it settled on the Western bourgeoisie with growing effect for the half-century following 1890.

It had a forerunner in Malthus (1766–1834), who had yet differed in many important respects from the later pessimists. The title of the first edition of his essay shows that it was composed largely to combat optimistic doctrines of progress: *An Essay on the Principle of Population, as it affects the Future Improvement of Society, with Remarks on the Speculations of Mr Godwin, M. Condorcet, and Other Writers* (1798). Yet as it appeared in an era of such expansion and self-confidence of bourgeois society, it was used less as a prophecy of gloom than as a guide of how to avoid disaster, and this increasingly became the view of the author also. It was left to later, more pessimistic ages, to revive Malthusianism as a direct threat to the future.

The propositions which Malthus set out to prove were that –

(1) Population is necessarily limited by the means of subsistence.
(2) Population invariably increases where the means of subsistence increase, unless prevented by some very powerful and obvious check.
(3) These checks ... are all resolvable into moral restraint, vice and misery.[11]

The pessimism lies in the last three words, for they imply, to turn Malthus's phrasing round, that unless there is moral restraint, there will always have to be vice and misery to restrict the numbers of the population to the means of feeding them.

The doctrine was not entirely new, and had been propounded, in all its essentials, by Robert Wallace more than a generation earlier; moreover, it is not so much a view of history as a simple logical deduction from certain premises that were widely dis-

11. *Principle of Population* (6th edn 1826, repr. 1890), pp. 2, 14.

puted then and have been proved wrong by the history of the following hundred and fifty years. Above all, the thesis was so badly formulated that it had to be drastically revised in later editions. If it nevertheless enjoyed an immense vogue and became part of the stock of all social thinking in the nineteenth century, it was because it completed the economic theory which the middle classes then found convenient, and provided a moral fig-leaf for the situation in which they became richer while the poor stayed in their poverty, while having to work harder and in increasingly less congenial conditions, held down by the detested New Poor Law.

But Malthus was, in fact, far closer to the thinking of the Enlightenment and its belief in progress than his middle-class popularizers allowed. He was incensed more by Condorcet's godlessness, his *hubris* and denial of original sin, than by his hope for salvation, and like Hume, he was concerned with the stimuli which would induce naturally indolent men to undergo the exertions and the rational risk-taking which alone would ensure progress. The main contrast with eighteenth-century optimism was that Malthus (a year or two after one of the worst harvests and near-famines of the century) was impressed less with the bounty than the niggardliness of nature, a view which he imparted to Ricardo, and in this way to classical economics, as well as to his disciples, Charles Darwin and Alfred Russell Wallace. If Godwin picked on Malthus's weakness at once by asserting that man would come to act more rationally and to exercise more prudence, to save himself from misery and vice, the later Malthus essentially agreed, and protested that he merely wished to aid man's positive action towards this progress –

On the whole . . . [his book concludes], though our future prospects respecting the mitigation of the evils arising from the principle of population may not be so bright as we could wish, yet they are far from being entirely disheartening, and by no means preclude [the gradual and progressive improvement of human society] . . . Although we cannot expect that the virtue and happiness of mankind will keep pace with that brilliant career of physical discovery; yet, if we are not wanting in ourselves, we may confidently indulge the hope that, to no unimportant extent, they will be influenced by its progress and will partake in its success.[12]

Thus a self-confident age casts even a potentially pessimistic theory, and a man fearful by nature, into an optimistic mould. By the end of the century, however, the self-confidence of the middle classes had been greatly sapped. From below, socialism threatened political power, and men like Ruskin and Morris, Tolstoy and Dostoyevsky attacked the very values on which progress was defended. From outside Europe, the coloured races stood as silent accusers and distant menaces. The World War and the depression deepened the despair. Reinhold Niebuhr expressed a widespread feeling when he warned in 1940 that –

History does not move forward without catastrophe, happiness is not guaranteed by the multiplication of physical comforts, social harmony is not easily created by more intelligence, and human nature is not as good or as harmless as had been supposed.[14]

But for a doctrine of an actual historical decline there had to be more than doubt. There had to be certainty that the lessons of history and social science pointed to a downward turn, to follow on the undoubted upward move since the Middle Ages. Such theories, therefore, also had to be basically cyclical.

The first important such theory, developed by Oswald Spengler (1880–1936) in his *Decline of the West*, (1917–22) did, in fact, combine much of what was despairing and critical in the current spirit of the time. But Spengler did not use the world's growing knowledge of historical data to show up inconsistencies in theories of optimism; instead, he created far more sweeping generalizations of his own, based on a contempt for intellect, and

12. *Principle of Population*, pp. 543, 544. Also *Summary View of the Principle of Population* (1830).

13. Quoted in CLARK A. CHAMBERS, 'The Belief in Progress in Twentieth-Century America', *J. Hist. Id.*, 19 (1958), p. 211.

a belief in feeling and intuition. In this respect, he was very much part of that revolt against reason which affected a distinct sector of European society around the turn of the century, and brought forth the ideas of Freud, of Pareto, of Bergson, and of Sorel. The most obvious influence, and the influence Spengler was most eager to acknowledge next to that of Goethe, was that of Nietzsche (1844–1900). From Nietzsche he took the relativist, the temporally conditioned view of ethics, and the permanence of the overwhelming will to power, the call of the blood, the force and the right of superman to dominate his society.

Spengler denied the Enlightenment's assumption of a single stream of world history –

I see, in place of that empty figment of *one* linear history which can only be kept up by shutting one's eyes to the overwhelming multitude of the facts, the drama of a *number* of mighty cultures, each springing with primitive strength from the soil of a mother-region to which it remains firmly bound throughout its whole life-cycle; each stamping its material, its mankind, in *its own* image; each having *its own* idea, *its own* passions, *its own* life, will and feeling, *its own* death.

More than any contemporary, more even than Max Weber (1864–1920), he believed each culture to have its own character, its own particular view of the world, and basic philosophy of life, of art, of science and religion, to the extent of making mutual understanding between any two of them impossible. The separate civilizations may thus use the same words, or outwardly the same concepts and institutions, but their inner meaning, to be sensed only by intuition, would be quite different. It was the business of the historian to discover

the morphological relationship that inwardly binds together the expression-forms of all branches of culture,

including

politics, ... mathematics, the measuring of their early ornamentation, the basic forms of their architecture, philosophies, dramas and lyrics.[14]

There had been some seven such civilizations in the past, including the Egyptian, Babylonian, Arab (or Magian), Classical, Indian, Chinese and Western (or Faustian); plus the Mexican, cut off before its full development, the Russian, which had not yet properly begun, and others struggling to be born but thwarted by overlying superior cultures, a phenomenon he called 'pseudomorphosis'. The list of civilizations has obvious similarities with that of Danilevski (1822–85) before him, and that of Toynbee after, and was used by all of them for comparable purposes.

The development of each of these civilizations is strikingly similar, or 'homologous', and Spengler even drew up elaborate charts to show the recurrence of certain events at almost exactly the same time-span after the beginning of each. Although Spengler denied from time to time that these time-spans were to be taken too literally, a thousand years being the allotted time for a civilization only in the sense that seventy years was that of a man, yet he held quite strongly to the predictive powers that his analogy gave him. Thus

the nineteenth and twentieth centuries, hitherto looked on as the highest point of an ascending straight line of world history, are in reality a stage of life which may be observed in every Culture that has ripened to its limit ... He who does not understand that this outcome [of the end of Western Culture] is obligatory and insusceptible of modification ... must forego all desire to comprehend history, to live through history or to make history.

The present, Western or 'Faustian' culture, is marked by external restlessness, by dynamic movement, by the striving after infinity, the hopeless search for the unattainable. It is also the most individualist civilization, and the most historical in outlook. It has its own 'specific and peculiar sort of history' derived

14. *Decline of the West*, I (English edn 1926), 21, 6–7.

from its idiosyncrasies, but it has also run through the same stages as all the others. Beginning in the tenth century (so that, if a millennium is the normal span, it had clearly almost run its course), it had passed through its medieval spring, its summer characterized by the Renaissance and the Reformation, its autumn of the Enlightenment and was now in the deep winter of nineteenth-century artistic infertility and socialist cynicism. One more stage was –

. . . still in store for us, and with [it] the history of West-European mankind will be definitely closed . . . The future of the West is not a limitless tending upwards and onwards for all time towards our present ideals, but a single phenomenon of history, strictly limited and defined as to form and duration, which covers a few centuries and can be viewed and, in essentials, calculated from available precedents.[15]

Its fate, to decline and perish in the foreseeable future, is inexorable.

When accused of hopeless pessimism, Spengler retorted that, on the contrary, he alone had the understanding of history to deal effectively and positively with the next phase of the West, though admittedly it was its final phase. He saw two possible approaches to an understanding of history, typified by the following pairs of contrasts or opposites: time-space, existence-consciousness, totem-taboo, culture-civilization, nobility-priesthood, 'destiny-men'-'causality-men', country-town, passion-understanding. In each, he favoured the first, more basic, more primitive, less rational alternative, and therefore deplored the rationalism and intellectualism, the doubts and materialistic views, the misplaced kindness to the masses of the nineteenth century. For the next phase, he wanted to place in their stead the simple and direct, military, powerful and wilful man, the nobleman and the man chosen by nature to rule. In

15. *Decline of the West*, I, 39, 38, 131, 38, 39.

the 1920s, when he made fitful attempts to enter politics, he looked benevolently on Mussolini's Fascist take-over as a dress rehearsal for the next phase; but it would be the Germans, opposing their freshness to the tiredness of the Anglo-Saxons, opposing discipline to freedom and authority to money, who would assume control.

There is in Spengler no reasoning behind the description of his historical drama, no explanation why within each civilization one stage should follow another, not even in the primitive form presented, for example, by Adam Ferguson, that luxury and widespread culture and education may tend to kill originality and weaken the will to fight, and may lead to debauch and decline. There is, in fact, no motor either in social or in individual psychological terms that Spengler might claim to have discovered, and of course there is no ethics and no teleology. There are merely the sequences, observed in other cultures, and to understand an age, or the cosmic forces that drive it, we have to 'feel', to grasp intuitively, and to sense instinctively.

Spengler expressed the deep-felt doubts and anxieties of his age, particularly during and immediately after the war. The striking similarity with the basic Nazi ideology is too close to be fortuitous, though in point of fact Spengler differed so much in minor detail as to fall foul of the Hitler administration in the last years of his life. His impact on other historians and philosophers was minimal. Most mocked his appalling ignorance or his simple-minded tendency to personify countries and societies, and to speak of the U.S.A., for example, as a tired and barren community. Many also noted his inability to see that science and technology had made of the modern West a society with a power and a world control for which there could be no conceivable parallel in the past.

There was one young historian in England, however, who felt when reading Spengler that his own ideas, his own plan of work, had been anticipated to such an extent that he even wondered briefly if there was much left for him to do –

As I read those pages teeming with firefly flashes of historical insight, I wondered at first whether my whole inquiry had been disposed of by Spengler before even the questions, not to speak of the answers, had fully taken shape in my mind.[16]

In the event, and after a lifetime's work, there was much to distinguish the theories of Arnold Toynbee (b. 1889) from those of Spengler, but there were also many striking similarities. Both look upon cultures or civilizations as the units or *personae* of history, though Toynbee enumerates many more, some twenty-one in all of which four were stillborn and eight were still operating, all of which makes the 'obviousness' of the unit less convincing. Both claim to have discovered a regular pattern of emergence, growth, decline and disintegration for each civilization, with the natural corollary that Western civilization, now long past its prime, will also follow precedents and decay in the foreseeable future. And both also have the kind of orderly, pigeon-holing rather than analytical mind which seeks to prove by even the minutiae of history – mosaics in the case of Spengler, for instance, and head-dress in that of Toynbee – that their categories are absolute determinants for all aspects of social life.

Toynbee's *magnum opus*, his ten volumes of *A Study of History* of which three appeared in 1934, three in 1939 and four in 1954 (plus two more volumes of maps and 'Reconsiderations'), show the kind of massive scholarship which is bound to impress, his prose style, while less epic than Spengler's, is more meaningful, and he is altogether more temperate, more reasonable in his approach to opponents, and, being basically religious, more concerned with ethical values. But he is just as committed, just as eager to be accepted as a prophet and to influence immediate practical policy. Toynbee's preoccupation with other civilizations, his attempt to put the West in its place, has become particularly appropriate since 1945, when the rest of the world has been successfully enforcing its claim to equality.

16. A. J. TOYNBEE, *Civilization on Trial* (1948), p. 12.

At the same time, however, it has made the arbitrariness of defining 'civilizations' as the basic entities, affecting every aspect of the character of their societies, more vulnerable. Not only does it make the deliberate neglect of technological or economic history, which would clearly cut across their boundaries, less tolerable; it has been plainly disproved by the experience of the 1950s and 1960s which has shown not only the renewed vitality of the West, but the desperate eagernesss of all other cultures to sink much of their identity in copying all its essential features.

Toynbee's civilizations, like the cultures of Spengler, follow a set pattern of growth and decline, in recognizable stages which are common, in similar sequences and similar time-spans, to all of them. Thus Toynbee felt that he and Thucydides were not separated by worlds called 'ancient' and 'modern', but were, on the contrary, 'philosophically contemporary'. This, incidentally, meant that he did not, like Spengler, believe that inter-communication at any depth between different civilizations was impossible. Indeed, the meeting of minds was easy across the same stage, because each civilization inexorably repeats the experience of the last, though each still has a different dominant collective personality.

Like Spengler's view, however, is Toynbee's élitist conception of historical dynamics: history is made by the 'creative minority', impinging on the inert or imitative masses, the 'internal proletariat' at home, and the 'external proletariat' abroad. But his élite is the middle class –

Today, in 1947, the Western middle class which, fifty years ago, was sitting carefree on the volcano's crust, is suffering something like the tribulation which, a hundred to a hundred and fifty years ago, was inflicted by Juggernaut's car on the English industrial working class ... The future of the Western middle class is in questions now in all Western countries; but the outcome is not simply the concern of the small fraction of mankind directly affected; for this Western middle class – this tiny minority – is the leaven that in recent times has leavened the lump and has thereby created the modern world. ... What is a crisis for this key minority is inevitably also a crisis for the rest of the world.[17]

At first glance it appears that Toynbee also has a motor, an internal mechanism which allows us to go beyond the observed sequences and to state, in terms of other generalizations, *why* one particular phase should follow another. This is the mechanism of 'challenge and response'. Thus, at the beginning of each civilization, the creative minority finds conditions that present a challenge – but not too daunting a one. It responds, solving its problems, and similarly meets the next challenge and the next. In this process, slowly and inevitably, a civilization grows and develops. Its growth is not to be thought of in technical terms, or in growing mastery over the physical environment, but in a cumulative inward self-determination or self-articulation, a growing refinement of the society's purposes and organization, accompanied by continuously successful 'responses' to challenges, continuing identification of the masses with the élite, and therefore a continuing unity of the civilization.

When the creative minority fails to respond to the challenges facing the society, civilizations begin to decline. The minority then has to rule by force, rather than by merit and consent, and social unity disintegrates as the 'proletariat' turns away from its leadership. The declining phase of each civilization is marked by class warfare, both against the internal proletariat and the external, that is inferior neighbouring societies who have come under the influence of the leading culture. The normal decline of a civilization occurs in a rhythm of three and a half beats, each with certain very significant accompanying characteristics. The so-called 'rout', or 'times of troubles', followed by a rally, or temporary peace; a relapse, saved by a second rally, in which the 'universal state' emerges; a second relapse, within the universal state, followed by a final rally and the death of the civilization.

17. *Civilization on Trial*, pp. 20–21.

At each challenge, the response becomes weaker, until there is no power left to react. But the destroyed élite, being in its later states a dominant, rather than a creative minority, has left behind a system of laws and administrative techniques, while the internal proletariat may have retired from this world to create the vision of a new one, and helped religion on to a higher stage in the next cycle. This raising of the level of religious consciousness is the final and essential purpose of civilization. It may be noted in passing that the quest of the masses in the last stages of civilization, such as, for example, in contemporary Europe, for Messianic salvation, for mysticism and religiosity, and in opposition to Utilitarianism, worldly happiness, rational, urban, intellectual and technological prowess, which Toynbee characterizes in his 'Universal Church', corresponds most closely to Spengler's view of the nature of that stage.

As with Spengler's master pattern, it is much easier to see its applicability to the prototype of the classical civilization and the rise of Christianity, than to any of the other civilizations which it is also alleged to fit. Yet, in the first versions of the theory, the pre-war volumes, the parallel was quite rigid, and since the current Western civilization began its decline with the Renaissance (sic) and the total process takes around four hundred years, Toynbee was quite confidently claiming the power to predict the imminent demise of Western civilization. Even in the second version, Volumes 7–10 published in 1954, the correctness of the original pattern and diagnosis was upheld, with Nazi Germany as an obvious symptom and instrument of decline. Her failure to subdue and destroy Western liberal society, and thus fulfil Toynbee's prophecy, was put down to a series of accidents and mistakes. However, in that second version a certain margin of freedom was allowed to the West to delay the inevitable, and improve it with some positive action in the creation of a new religion, combining in a higher form elements of beliefs held in several present-day civilizations. Finally, the third version, Volume 12, entitled *Reconsiderations*, confessed that –

I have been at fault in having been content to operate with the Hellenic model [of civilization] only. Though this particular key has opened many doors, it has not proved omnicompetent.

Toynbee there recognizes at least three standard patterns, exemplified by the Hellenic, the Chinese and the Jewish civilizations.

While it is noble of a philosopher of history to admit to error, a theory loses much in value if cast in the form: there is an inevitable standard pattern of development, except where it can be shown to be different. It is weaker still as a motor of history, for Toynbee freely admits that there is no analytical reason for the sequences. There are merely repeatedly observed facts –

Pace Spengler, there seems to be no reason why a succession of stimulating challenges should not be met by a succession of victorious responses *ad infinitum*. On the other hand, when we make an empirical comparative study of the paths which the dead civilizations have respectively travelled from breakdown to dissolution, we do here seem to find a Spenglerian uniformity.[18]

Is this enough to lend any value to the 'challenge' and 'response' metaphor? Let us look upon it as a fairly extreme method of taking much for granted which other historians think worthy of discussion: the struggle for existence, technical progress, social cohesion; and to concentrate on what is often taken for granted by others: the physical environment, the positive response to too much, or too little difficulty in pursuing a multiplicity of individual, and therefore total social, aims. Then, taken literally, it asserts that societies meet difficulties, which they may, or may not, overcome. Since there has never been any suggestion of drawing up *a priori* or generalized rules as to when or on what terms difficulties may be too great to be overcome, the concept becomes merely a trivial truism.

There is the further problem of the post-war position of Toynbee. It maintains, on the one hand, that a lifelong study of twenty-two civilizations has established without any doubt

18. *A Study of History*, XII (1961), p. 186; *Civilization on Trial*, p. 12.

that a certain pattern will emerge in each, precisely because, in its declining stages, the civilization is unable to respond sufficiently well to its challenges. Simultaneously, it assures us that by following his advice in creating an amalgam-religion there is a way in which the present civilization can respond, and thus the pattern can be broken, and the inevitable disaster delayed or averted.

Among Toynbee's more detailed statements, the proposition that the Western world has been in decline since the Renaissance has been one of the most controversial and has offended most convictions. It is vital for an understanding of Toynbee to see why he opposes the clear consensus of his age in this respect.

Basically, Toynbee is opposed to rationalism. It is no accident that for him, as for Spengler and others, pessimism about the future is combined with distrust of the power of reason: both stem from the same despair (no matter how little understood consciously) of the future of one's own class. If the rules of a rational understanding of history point in an undesirable direction, the rules must be wrong, and we must seek refuge from reality in myth. In one way, the whole of the splendid and massive labours of Toynbee may be looked upon as a backing for his myth, rather than as the raw material out of which the myth was created. Toynbee is instinctively opposed to all that liberalism stands for: freedom to differ, a pluralist society, suspicion of authority, a belief in the values of this life, pursued by rational means, within ethical concepts justifiable on human rather than mythological or divine terms. Toynbee, on the contrary, prefers feeling and intuition to analysis; a monolithic God to a pluralistic society; fixed, chartered course to chance or human initiative; and a miracle to partial, piecemeal reform.

For these ideals, the Christian medieval society, or rather Toynbee's idealized version of it (seen moreover from the high point of the castle rather than from that of the serf's hovel) was the last concrete expression in Europe. Then, it is alleged, there was unity and obedience in Europe, there was only one religion, and it dominated men's lives. Since then there has been a continuous decline into questions, doubts and disagreements, into experimentation and wilfulness. On the pattern of earlier civilizations, the next stage would be the 'universal state' of a higher religion. To fulfil our purpose, this will necessarily have to be an amalgam of the best of the existing religions, and will then become the base for the next civilization.

For Toynbee's civilizations are, as it were, on an ascending plane. There have been, so far, three levels of civilization, each deriving something from its 'parent' or transmitting something to its successor. Thus the first generation group included the Egyptian, Minoan, and Indus civilizations; the second, the Babylonian, Hellenic and Indic; and the third generation, the Western, Eastern Orthodox and Hindu civilizations. In this way Toynbee found it possible to combine the Jewish-Zoroastrian view of history, postulating an upward move, with the Graeco-Indian belief in endlessly repetitive cycles. If we put religion, not civilization, first –

we shall have to think of the civilizations of the second generations as having come into existence ... in order to provide an opportunity for fully-fledged higher religions to come to birth ... in the same line of thought, we shall have to think of primary civilizations [as having] accomplished their mission indirectly by giving birth to secondary civilizations, out of which the fully fledged higher civilizations did eventually arise.

On this reading, the history of Religion appears to be unitary and progressive by contrast with the multiplicity and repetitiveness of the histories of civilizations ...

If this view of the prospects of Religion were to carry conviction, it would open up a new view of the role of the civilizations. If the movement of the chariot of Religion were constant in its direction the cyclic and recurrent movement of the rises and falls of civilizations might ... serve its purpose, and find its significance, in promoting the chariot's ascent towards Heaven by periodic revolutions on Earth of 'the sorrowful wheel' of birth-death-birth.

After all, if a vehicle is to move forward on a course which its driver has set, it must be borne along on wheels that turn monotonously round and round. While civilizations rise and fall and, in falling, give rise to others, some purposeful enterprise, higher than theirs, may all the time be making headway, and in a divine plan, the learning that comes through the suffering caused by the failures of civilizations may be the sovereign means of progress.[19]

The next fourth-level civilization will take the best of all the four higher religions (with a strong preference for the Roman Catholic version) and turn them into one super-religion. This, no doubt, is the purpose of human history.

The selection of these four 'higher religions', to the exclusion, for example, of Judaism, for which Toynbee has an irrational aversion is as arbitrary as the selection of the 'civilizations' themselves, and few would today subscribe to the thesis that the signs of the times point to a worldwide religious initiative. But, at least, the prospect is strikingly more hopeful than in the first six volumes. Though he was reluctant to admit it, the liberal, rational West had not been defeated and had shown plenty of life and recuperative power in the 1940s and 1950s. What was more to the point, Toynbee's own society appeared to have gained a new lease of life. Capitalism, after all, survives and shows very strong growth potential, and on the basis of this satisfactory performance, much of the internecine struggle in the Western world is, at least, temporarily, submerged, although now the failure to benefit the coloured world may pose a threat to the West.

And so, in recent years, we have heard less of synthetic religions and dying civilizations, and much more of the concrete, but this time soluble, problems of the West, and the challenge of the underdeveloped world. It is, at times, as if the volumes on the *Study of History* had never been written. In strong contrast

19. D. C. SOMERVELL, *A Study of History*, by *A. J. Toynbee. Abridgement* (2 vols., 1946, 1957), II, 87–9, 92; *Civilization on Trial*, p. 15.

to that study, we now find, for example, a much greater positive role given to the rise of technology and the consequent growth of material wealth. There is also the recognition that the wish to imitate the West in these respects is moulding all the other surviving civilizations into a Western pattern – though Toynbee would insist that this global imitation is for the sake of matching Western power, rather than because of the separate wishes of millions of individuals to better their own material conditions of life. Indeed, he is now willing to admit that the representatives of these other, non-Western civilizations, instead of merely borrowing the technology, but in other respects keeping to the logic and main ideas of their own cultures, as his theories would assume, in fact do accept more and more of the values of the West also. Everywhere middle classes are being created, transforming their own traditional societies in the Western image, both in the sense of their economic efficiency and their social justice –

There is a movement on foot for giving the benefits of civilization to that huge majority of the human race that has paid for civilization without sharing in its benefits, during the first five thousand years of civilization's existence.

Since the dawn of civilization, about 5,000 years ago, the world's peasantry has carried the load of civilization on its back without receiving any appreciable share in civilization's benefits. These benefits have been monopolized by a tiny privileged minority, and, until yesterday, this injustice was inevitable ... In our time, technology is within sight of being able to produce enough of civilization's material benefits to provide for the whole human race ... At last, the majority is shaking off the fatalism that has been paralysing it since the beginning of time. It is becoming alive to the truth that an improvement in its lot is now possible. More than that, it is realizing that it can do something towards this by its own efforts.[20]

20. TOYNBEE, *The Present-Day Experiment in Western Civilization* (1962), pp. 36–7; *The Economy of the Western Hemisphere* (1962), pp. 1, 3–4; *America and the World Revolution* (1962), pp. 9, 10.

Thus technology, and the social organization by which alone it can be applied, has led civilizations which once he thought to be the separate and distinct units of history, to merge into each other; the present age, which once had numerous parallels in other civilizations at similar stages, is unique in offering a modicum of wealth to all; the middle classes, once thought of as presiding over a decline going back to the Renaissance, have still plenty of creative life in them; and there is some salvation in social justice rather than in religious myth. It is a remarkable conversion. What caused it? It is hard to avoid the view that the success of the liberal, bourgeois West in the war of 1939–45, in its economic recovery since, and in leading the development and industrialization of much of the rest of the world, has given hope to one who had come to believe that the role of his society and his class was played out. It would perhaps be hard to find a more striking example of the effect of concrete experience and participation on a strongly held dogma in this field.

It might appear at first sight that the two groups of thinkers treated in this chapter are at opposite poles of thought, and that they have nothing in common save a disbelief in progress and a denial of the values built up by the liberal Enlightenment in the eighteenth century and the socialist conscience of the nineteenth – the 'progressive' movements of their time. Yet their opposition to these values takes forms which, despite their superficial opposition, give them a unity at a deeper level. This can, perhaps, best be illustrated by the thought of Karl Mannheim (1893–1947) who combined much that was most fundamental to both.

Mannheim's system of thought, as propounded in his main work, *Ideology and Utopia* (1929, English edn 1936) has come to be called the 'sociology of knowledge'. It is as much a product of its author's experience as the other literature reviewed here. 'It is doubtful', wrote the editor of the English edition –

whether such a book as this could have been written in any other period, for the issues with which it deals, fundamental as they are, could only be raised in a society and in an epoch marked by profound social and intellectual upheaval.

It is based on the assertion that all historical truth, all reasoning applied to human history, is relative. It is evident, he states –

that (a) every formulation of a problem is made possible only by a previous actual human experience which involves such a problem; (b) in selection from a multiplicity of data there is involved an act of will on the part of the knower; and (c) forces arising out of living experience are significant in the direction which the treatment of the problem follows.

Moreover, this applies equally to the attitude of a whole society towards a problem –

Every epoch has its fundamentally new approach and its characteristic point of view, and consequently sees the 'same' object from a new perspective.

Finally, it is true not merely for history, but also for other fields –

. . . the historico-social process is of essential significance for most of the domains of knowledge.[21]

Here, however, we are largely concerned with this view in relation to history.

It will be evident at once that this echoes closely the view of Spengler who thought that not only religion, philosophy, social science and the arts, but even natural science and mathematics were different for each civilization and different for each nationality, to the extent that communication and understanding across the barrier of civilizations were impossible. Similarly, it was Toynbee's contention that all historical thought was inevitably relative to the historians' time and place.

Mannheim's significant agreement with the pessimists who believe that Western civilization is in an advanced stage of de-

21. LOUIS WIRTH, Preface to *Ideology and Utopia*, p. xvii, and pp. 240, 243.

cline (for which belief this form of historical relativism would not, at first sight, appear to be essential) is matched by his agreement with them over the futility of liberal and 'progressive' hopes. The conviction which the Enlightenment and its successors had, that they had found a science in history and, with it, a key to progress, was pure illusion. It arose from their background, their social habitat, their biased 'total ideology', which they mistook for a scientific point of view, but which was only a partial truth. Thus all historic 'truths' bear marks of their partial origins; historians looking at the same events from different viewpoints are bound to come to different conclusions, for, try as they might (and most of them are not even aware of their inevitable bias), they cannot eliminate a residual activist element. This is particularly so in history, where we study the action of men, and therefore have to enter into men's motives. To do this, it is imperative to absorb first of all the whole of the assumptions of their age and their class, to be, as it were, on the 'inside' of phenomena. This insight, or sympathetic introspection, is the core of the social-historical method. But at the same time there cannot be any pure thought on the part of the observer. Thought emerges as part of the shaping of events, the ends of action are never fully discoverable until the act is finished, and the observer is part of the observed. An objective, detached, scientific appraisal of social events therefore is a feat which is beyond human capacity. In default of it, we must give all views equal value, and refuse to choose a 'correct' one among them.

It is true that Mannheim admits that by allowing for the bias, intellectuals who are in any case not tied too closely to current class interests, may come much closer to 'the truth', and it is the contribution of the sociology of knowledge to encourage as far as possible the shedding of the temporal bias. Moreover, by denying that we can have a rational understanding of historical events, he does not necessarily imply that the events themselves are irrational, or unknowable, by a superhuman science. Yet the import, the direct effort of Mannheim's theory is to combine the views of those who hold that each civilization is an organism of its own, with a divisive force stronger than the unifying force of humanity, and that each civilization must inevitably die in the manner in which civilizations of the past have died.

The revolt, then, is against rationalism, against knowledge, against science in history. If we have no knowledge of what is true, we can have no knowledge of what is moral. There can be no absolute morality outside the historical period, the historical bias, operative at any given time. There can be no standards, no valid rules of social conduct, against which to measure any action, since what is good or bad, desirable or undesirable, even effective and ineffective, depends entirely on the point of view. The flight from rationality is also a flight from moral obligation to society, and both are equally characteristic of those who fear that the historic role of their class is at an end.

With the decline in the belief of supernatural sanctions, which began with the Enlightenment, it has, indeed, become much harder to find a firm resting place, a fixed point on which a moral system or a social objective greater than the individual can be built up. What is a crime from one point of view, is heroic self-sacrifice from another, and all the civic virtues of one system become persecuted vices over the border, where political power is built on a different class structure. In this ocean of restless waves there has emerged only one firm island outside the temporal and biased perspective of each separate interest: the continuous improvement, that is to say, the progress of humanity itself. It is a yardstick against which the separate contributions of men, of classes, and of theories, can be measured, and it can give moral reassurance to those who are well aware of the relativity of their convictions, but who yet require, psychologically, the assurance of a firmer morality. Conversely, without the conviction of progress, there is no alternative to an inevitable despair in reason and in a rational, scientific approach to society, and to the decline into the mythology of nihilism.

CHAPTER FIVE

THE CHALLENGE OF
PROGRESS TODAY

IN the years since the end of the Second World War, the conversion of the world's mood towards human progress has been quite startling in its extent from the depth of the despair of the generation after 1914. The doubters and the pessimists who had formed an interesting, rather than a significant, sector of European opinion in the 1890s, appeared to have been vindicated when two great wars, and a destructive peace separating them, threatened the values and the very civilization on which earlier hopes of continuous progress had been built. With these calamities staring them in the face, many began to feel that the easy optimism of the nineteenth century was no longer a view that could reasonably be held.

It is important to stress that the pessimism was derived not from any powerful new theories, but from the historical experience. Men had seen the veneer of civilized behaviour stripped off in wartime and the pointless slaughter of millions go on year after year, while politicians displayed their utter inability to control their nation's destiny. The mind of a whole generation was scarred by the patent futilities of mass unemployment, the collapse of banks, of stock exchanges, and of world commodity prices, while splendid technical powers of production lay idle or were used for destructive purposes. And it could be sensed widely that the weakness of the resistance to the Fascist dictators, first within their own countries and then by the remaining liberal powers, reflected the paralysis of will of the middle classes, who had carried European civilization up to that point. They now had lost confidence in their own future, and were reluctant to opt for either Communism or the new barbarism, which appeared the only alternatives open to them.

And then the second war greatly stimulated a revival of belief in the ideas of the Enlightenment, and at its end, somewhat to its surprise, the West found itself on a steeply rising curve of material prosperity, technical innovation and social peace such as it had not even conceived possible in the 1930s. Men, perhaps fortunately, easily forget the ill, and take the good for granted, and with striking speed, the former belief in progress was disinterred, refurbished, and began to shine forth as if it had never been in any danger.

Let us be clear both about the nature, and the causes, of this phenomenon. After decades of destructiveness, when the centuries-old promise of science and rationalism appeared to have been broken, and political or social factors seemed once again to have combined, in the face of an advancing technology, to make men tear each other to pieces, and perhaps repeat, at a level so much higher than it had once been considered safe, the grim experience of the Roman Empire, the cloud is suddenly lifted once more. Societies are making the most of their resources, and wealth advances almost everywhere as fast as technology and resources allow. The major powers have avoided war, and are collaborating in areas in which their differing ideologies makes such collaboration hardly credible. The lion is lying down with the lamb, and such earlier terrors of the liberal West as Japan or Germany are vying with the best of them in the peaceful uses of technology, in moderate home and foreign policies, in liberal-democratic government and in aid, rather than domination, towards weaker neighbours. No country is excluded today: all, in Africa, Asia, in the Western Hemisphere or on Pacific Islands, have at least a claim to a share of the cornucopia. Objectively speaking, a Condorcet or a Godwin might not be dissatisfied, were he to visit the world today.

Moreover, this very material success has removed much of the tension and made possible a much more human attitude within societies. Growing wealth permits, as a minimum, a sharing of the benefits with hitherto submerged groups, and in many countries welfare policies have gone much further. Even if there is injustice or resentment, they are easier to bear if things are getting better. No extremist, irrational, humanity-denying mass movement can flourish, as long as some of men's real demands can be met and as long as there is hope that a rational approach can deliver at least some of the goods without major destruction of existing institutions. Put at its crudest, the haves can afford to give something away, and the have-nots can see improvements ahead even in the existing framework.

The result of this more hopeful reality and of the mental habits which it necessarily engenders, has been that the world has again resumed the optimistic stance it occupied over much of the nineteenth century. Socialist philosophy, now as then, still demands social revolution as a necessary precondition of progress, and bourgeois philosophy still maintains that the greatest hope lies with the maintenance of the present framework, but both equally believe in a happier destiny of mankind. Observing the power of the new science and technology, and the growing social control made possible by it, they also both share the earlier faith in the growing possibility of the humanity of man towards his fellow men.

The striking nature of the reconversion of the world to the belief in progress is perhaps best brought out by the divergent attitudes of economists on the one hand, and historian-philosophers on the other. That divergence existed also during the Industrial Revolution, but then it was the philosophers of history who were assured of unending progress, while the economists believed that humanity had reached its ideal social framework, and that within it only limited growth was possible, which was then, as like as not, going to end in the stagnation of a 'stationary state' –

Long after Adam Smith, the literature of economics is strewn with prophecies of a stationary state in which growth would finally cease under the influence of some limiting factor such as population growth, the law of diminishing returns, a fuel shortage or a chronic tendency to over-save ... The main shift of opinion [Cairncross goes on to say] did not take place until the war and post-war years.[1]

Now, in the post-war years, the roles have become reversed. It is among political philosophers and philosophers of history that doubts remain, doubts nourished on the ideas of the destructive decades before, and running on now, particularly in academic circles somewhat isolated from social realities. By contrast, it is the economists who have plunged fully into the stream of progress. Their unquestioning certainty of its existence, with but few exceptions, has allowed them to concentrate single-mindedly on the means of achieving it. Most of them have absorbed in their work also the unspoken assumption that growing wealth and the social changes which are its preconditions, will themselves ensure improvements in the other aspects of social life which together make up the 'progress' of humanity.

The post-war preoccupation of economists with economic progress falls into two distinct parts, which have led to the creation of two new areas of study, although there are many links, particularly of a theoretical nature, between them. One, often designated 'economic growth', is concerned with the continuous increase in wealth in the advanced countries and normally does not pose as a prerequisite a major social change in the class structure, though it may imply the adaptation of many individual institutions. The other, often described as 'economic development', deals with the path of traditional and 'underdeveloped' economies towards the industrialized Western type of society. This is always taken to imply a revolutionary change, not only in the economic sphere, but also in class structure, in ideology and 'motivation', in social relations and religion, and in numerous other spheres.

The first recalls the attitude of the 'classical' political economists in the period of the Industrial Revolution, but with a difference of degree so great as almost to amount to a difference in

1. A. K. CAIRNCROSS, *Factors in Economic Development* (1962, paperback edn 1964), p. 14.

kind. Compared with any earlier period, economic growth in the decades since 1945 has been much faster in the West, and this is almost inevitable, since growth is based on better techniques, and science and technology have been changing and expanding incomparably faster in recent years. Indeed, it can be argued that it is the peculiarly close linkage between theoretical science and practical or applied technology which has made the last twenty or twenty-five years so successful technologically. At the same time, the speed of change requires social and even individual adjustments, for example in skills, which may prove more difficult to sustain even than those of the Industrial Revolution.

More interesting, however, is the assumption of the inevitability of 'economic development' in the Western sense, among the large majority of the world's population living in 'underdeveloped' economies. For one thing, it is basically new. Even a generation ago, Spengler and Toynbee could argue, with at least some plausibility, that India, China, the Arab world, or the Russian world, were so different in their total basic outlook as to make communication across the frontiers meaningless, if not impossible. Toynbee has lived long enough to see his mistake (*see* page 180 above). It is important to stress how much the assumption, now accepted as self-evident, that every country will 'progress', mainly in the economic sphere but also in all other sociohistorical respects, towards the Western model, contradicts fundamentally the doubters and pessimists, and how much and how startlingly it vindicates the prophets of progress –

For some fifty years the world – East and West, capitalist and communist, democratic and more democratic ... has been engaged in what it has agreed to call economic development ... It has been easy to assume that the industrial apparatus of the United States, Western Europe, and the U.S.S.R. is the natural and indeed the only model for the new countries. They need only to recreate in some rough form what the more developed countries already have. Development is the faithful imitation of the developed.

It is particularly significant that while Galbraith is anxious to show that for technical reasons the path of new countries might be different, he nevertheless admits the close parallel with the Western industrial revolutions –

The occasion is the same ... The new countries of Asia and Africa are now concerned, as were those of Western Europe, in the late eighteenth and early nineteenth centuries, with understanding the processes on which progress depends ... The nineteenth century discussion was in a world that was rather proud of what was happening. The twentieth century discussion is in a world where much has happened but which feels that a great deal more must happen and very soon.[2]

Whilst some historians still proclaim their doubt in progress, the large majority of the world assumes that it is bound to occur, and takes major steps to see that it does. Among economists and specialists in closely related fields, the attention devoted to economic 'development' is among the outstanding facts of the age, driven as it is by the political and economic demands of the affected societies themselves. The bookshelves are groaning under the publications on the topic. One *select* list, for publications in English only, dealing with development, and published between the war and 1958, has 1,027 entries (books and articles); a supplement for 1958–62, again in the English language alone, lists another 732 entries.[3] A whole series of new academic journals now covers the subject, including such highly reputable periodicals as *The Journal of Development Studies, The Journal of Developing Areas, Economic Development and Cultural Change, The International Development Review*, and *Comparative Studies in Society and History* – to name some

2. J. K. GALBRAITH, *Economic Development* (Cambridge, Mass., 1964), pp. 2–3, 37–8.

3. A. HAZLEWOOD, *The Economics of 'Under-Developed' Areas. An Annotated Reading List* (1964). ELOISE G. REQUA and JANE STATHAM, *The Developing Nations: A Guide to Information Sources* (Detroit, 1965), has 220 pages of titles, excluding bibliographies, on the subject.

English-language ones alone. In all this contribution to knowledge, scarcely a single page questions whether countries of so many different historical backgrounds are historically justified in wishing to follow the pattern of progress set by the West. At the same time, this avalanche of words and ideas is, as if by a miracle, kept out of the large and growing literature on 'progress' in history, with which much of this book has been concerned.

It may be argued that the two have little in common, and that the wish of poverty-stricken, diseased and exploited populations, to enjoy the relative comfort and security of the citizens of the U.S.A., has little to do with the laws of history or the future destiny of the world. The wish to catch up with the West is, indeed, not identical with the belief that humanity faces an unending prospect of further 'progress'. But the assumptions on which both are based are so similar, and the dividing line between them is so blurred, that it is difficult to hold to one, yet deny the other. Among the common assumptions are the beliefs that (no matter how divergent their history in earlier ages), the modern stages are basically identical, and therefore predictable and plannable, for all humanity; that progress along this unilinear path of progress is both 'natural' and desirable; that once certain early steps are correctly taken, the developing societies will continue under their own steam, in inevitable 'self-sustaining' growth, and that growth will bring inevitably in its wake such other desirable developments as greater democracy, more education and a higher status in the international community, which will promote further growth. Even among the advanced countries, the richer, for example the U.S.A., are taken to mark out the next stage along the route of progress, and for these leaders in turn, it is clear that they are basically on the right road, creating ever greater material wealth, ever greater power over man's environment, ever more assistance for human physical and psychological frailties, and thereby the opportunity, which they cannot but believe will be taken, of ever higher personal fulfilment and achievement. There is similar agreement also to the converse proposition, that without economic growth and the social improvement which it makes possible, all hopes of any other 'progress' are doomed from the start.

It is worth stressing that this unanimity is very recent. Even in Russia, a country virtually inside the European orbit after Peter the Great, a large, influential and sensitive body of opinion held throughout the nineteenth century that the country's future did not lie in imitating the economically successful path of the West, but in finding her own. Further afield, almost into our present day, Gandhi attempted to lead his people in a different direction, and it could reasonably be argued that China and Japan might accept the technologies, but would never accept the ideologies, of the West, in their view of the future. All this has changed, and today Asiatics as well as Africans, Buddhists as well as pagans, Roman Catholics or Muslims accept Western 'development', whether in its American, or its Marxian, prototype.

With it, we have entered upon a new phase in the idea of progress, and the concrete experience on which it is built. From the late seventeenth century onwards, it was based on science and technology used to improve the performance of industry, and on the rise of the European middle classes. In the nineteenth, the working classes rose to self-consciousness and began to demand their own share of the inheritance, though still within the same Western framework of reference. Now the relation of forces has changed again. The extra-European world, denying its own history, has entered the picture, to strengthen the traditional conviction of progress, yet perhaps also, in the future, to modify it in its own direction. In the 'developed' countries, economic success in greatly changed circumstances, makes the middle classes again confident of maintaining progress within an unchanged class structure in Europe, thought its attitude to the rest of the world is ambivalent and there is doubt in their minds whether among those less favoured nations there might not, perhaps, be a need to change the social, political, legal and ideological superstructure as well before the levels of the West can be reached. By contrast, the heirs to the nineteenth-century socialist prophets of European progress have become demoralized, and are, with success all around them, more than half inclined to take the world as its own bourgeoisie presents it.

The socialist demoralization is therefore due to the renewed success of Western capitalism, rather than to the failure of socialism; on the contrary, the progress of 'socialist' countries in recent years has been so evident that it is accepted even by hostile observers. But it has been only too clear that this 'progress' is in the same direction as that in the West, even in the most extremist, and most clearly 'underdeveloped' of socialist countries, the People's Republic of China. The abolition of poverty and want, the check on diseases, the general mastery over man's environment, all demand complex social organization, and particularly large-scale manufacturing, transport, and research and development units using certain techniques. In turn, these require similar motivations, methods of employment and incentives to further progress, no matter what the actual political ideology of the State might be.

The growing similarity and apparent convergence of all modern societies, whether dedicated officially to free enterprise, to a mixed economy, or to socialism, has long since been noted by all acute observers. Similarly, there has been a remarkable convergence of ideals also, all systems claiming successes in the achievement of greater equality, democracy or human dignity. We need not concern ourselves here with the problem of how far the different systems of ownership and the class distribution of power will inhibit a total identification of all systems with each other, or rather, which present system approximates most closely, or is the best placed to develop into, the system demanded by the new technology and the new social relations associated with it. For our purposes it is sufficient to note that both the leading current philosophies that move nations are agreed on the assurance of continued progress in the advanced countries also. The Marxist countries still draw on the humanistic optimism which animated the progressive school of the first half of the nineteenth century. The West, epitomized by the U.S.A., has in its flush of self-confidence after the second Great War picked up again the optimistic strands of classical political economy. It may be true, as Galbraith observes, that there a belief in social change is not encouraged –

... the economic system of the United States is praised on all occasions of public ceremony as a largely perfect structure ... There is massive change but, except as the output of goods increases, all remains as before.[4]

Yet on the basis of that affluence, men have come to accept a future 'Utopia of abundance', the growing power of humanity over its environment and the enlargement of the life of man by the growing freedom over his own destiny. No matter if description of the economy, guided by ideological interest, pronounces the system perfect and therefore immutable; post-war experience has again revived, as strongly as ever, the belief in an endless vista of human progress.

Of course, there are misgivings, and the misgivings equally reflect our recent experience. For the belief that social engineering would keep pace with mechanical engineering, and that human barbarity would give way to civilized behaviour as soon as men were no longer hungry, disease-ridden and haunted by fear, was safe only as long as competent engineering and the conquest of hunger were themselves only Utopian hopes. Now that we are in a position to test these hypotheses, the results are not such as to give unqualified satisfaction. Sooner or later we must all face the facts of Belsen, and the facts of Hiroshima and Nagasaki and other, similar acts performed by the most advanced, 'civilized' and Christian nations of the West. The public, with its notoriously short memory, can afford to enjoy the new consumer spending spree, it can absorb as part of its gains some of

4. *The New Industrial State* (1967), p. 1.

the cultural heritage hitherto outside its reach, and it can register undoubted progress at that level. But below the surface there is the fact of unregenerate brutality and callousness, in virtually our own day, to deny in total the vision of Godwin and Condorcet.

Basically, the frightening experience of our own generation, the 'rediscovery of evil', has led many to the conviction that human nature does not change, or that the change is too slow to be perceptible if measured against the speed of technical change. Moreover, man's power for evil grows equally with his power for good, and the potential damage he may do grows with the potential benefits. Sooner or later, if the experience of the past may be called in evidence, he will use this power for evil, and this time, unlike all the past occasions, he will have the ability to destroy humanity.

Something of the primitive fear of the unknown has arisen with regard to progress itself. Progress, Huizinga wrote in the despairing decade of the 1930s, is

a highly ambiguous notion. For who knows but that a little further on the way a bridge may have collapsed or a crevice split the earth.[5]

The former dread of the barbarian from without –

the foreign causes that tend to raise, to depress, and sometimes to overwhelm a community

still expressed by Burke in 1796, had ended in the nineteenth century as it became clear that there were no unknown continents left, and Europe had nothing to fear from the military capability of those that were known. A hundred years after Burke, Engels could write placidly and with remarkable prescience of the

case of the conquest and brutal destruction of economic resources, by which, in certain circumstances, a whole local or national

5. *In the Shadow of Tomorrow. A Diagnosis of the Spiritual Distemper of our Time* (1936), p. 39.

economic development could formerly be ruined. Nowadays such a case usually has the opposite effect, at least among great nations: in the long run the defeated power often gains more economically, politically and morally than the victor.[6]

Today the fear is different, the fear of what is known, of what has been uncovered, from within society. There is an echo here of John Stuart Mill's doubts, to the effect that progress in his day meant largely

that kind of improvement only, which distinguishes a wealthy and powerful nation from savages and barbarians;

whilst in other respects, such as being 'more eminent in the best characteristics of Man and Society, farther advanced in the road to perfection; happier, nobler, wiser', his age might have been 'stationary, even retrograde'. Today, also –

we have come to see that orderly society and orderly change are neither natural nor normal, but rare and precarious achievements.

And the 'liberals', that is those who believed in secular progress, have had to sustain the hardest shocks –

It is a liberal historian who writes that the belief in human perfectibility left liberalism unprepared for Hitler,[7]

not only his barbaric actions, but also the denial of something more fundamental, namely the supremacy of reason, and the substitution for it of new mythology and obscurantism.

Consequently, many have looked for constraints on human power in order to constrain human evil. What might be called the 'Austrian school' has held fast to its doctrine that both progress and freedom are secured only by economic decentralization,

6. EDMUND BURKE, *Works* (ed. Earl Fitzwilliam and Sir Richard Bourke, 8 vols., 1852), V, 254; *Marx–Engels Correspondence* (1941), p 481, Engels to Conrad Schmidt, 27 October 1890. See also p. 164 above.

7. JOHN STUART MILL, 'Civilization' (1836), in *Dissertations and Discussions* (3 vols., 1859), I, 160–61; FRANKEL, *The Case for Modern Man* (1957), pp. 18, 24, 35.

by private enterprise and by competition. Socialism, the mental product of the 'envy-driven masses', will have to resort to tyranny and the destruction of all the painfully acquired liberties of nineteenth-century Europe when it imposes its imperfect solutions. The only hope is to revert to the enlightened self-interest of the Utilitarians, and let each man pursue his own interest, as the classical economists taught –

... there are no irreconcilable conflicts between selfishness and altruism, between economics and ethics, between the concerns of the individual and those of society.[8]

More powerful has been the Christian opposition to the idea of progress. Shattered by the achievements of science and rationalism, the Church has had little new to contribute to European thought until now, suddenly, the belief in original sin, and the need of an ethical anchor outside the historical framework of this world, appear to have become necessary. Some Churchmen are inclined to look favourably on hopes of earthly progress, and a few even look on them as Christian-inspired. Others view the belief in progress as a hostile force, since it appears to deny the power of Providence, it offers a competing teleology, and it is based on temporary systems of values. Dean Inge would admit progress only in

accumulating knowledge and experience and the instruments of living. For the rest, 'if it is progress to turn the fields and woods of Essex into East and West Ham, we may be thankful that progress is a sporadic and transient phenomenon of history.'[9]

Christian thinkers have, from time to time, raised their voices to warn against the danger that those whose ethics are based on the belief in progress, are too inclined to sacrifice the present generation to the welfare of future ones, and in this have usefully pointed to a common weakness. They have also, in a belated *riposte* to the Darwinists, stressed that evolution need not mean

8. L. VON MISES, *Theory and History* (1958 edn), pp. 54–5.
9. W. R. INGE, The *Idea of Progress* (Oxford, 1920), pp. 24, 14.

improvement. But for the most part they are attempting to stem a tide with means which, however well intentioned, are not suitable for the task. Maritain's demand for 'natural Platonism', for an external spiritual goal common to the whole of society, simply cannot be realized, for it would negate the experience of those he wishes to convert, and in any case agreement on ends does not necessarily lead to agreement as to means. Niebuhr, similarly a product of the modern dilemma, is even more destructive. Since original sin, the evil in man's nature, is permanent, the belief in progress is not only misguided, but also harmful. It

is responsible for the follies, self-deceptions, and arrogant hopes on which the modern era has misspent its energies.

The belief that when man progresses in knowledge he also progresses in virtue explains why science has been erected into a false Messiah.[10]

But his own solution of 'sin' explains nothing: there is nothing to be derived or learnt from the belief in sin that cannot be equally taught or defended without it.

A further interesting sidelight on the widespread doubt in the ability of frail humans to carry the vast powers of modern science and technology is furnished by science fiction. Its bias towards the catastrophic may be natural as the basis of a story, yet authors and readers do not have to strain their credulity to accept the convention of this type of literature that some groups of men will abuse the new powers, and that there will be no corresponding growth in man's moral goodness or sense of social responsibility, so that in those stories in which virtue is triumphant, the virtue consists exclusively of human qualities already existing today. Science fiction writers do not assume, as did the men of the Enlightenment, that technical progress will be accompanied by comparable moral progress.

How, then, can the modern optimist, conscious of the bitter

10. FRANKEL, pp. 43 ff, 75 ff.

lessons of the past two hundred years, and particularly of the past fifty, overcome his misgivings and hold to what must seem to him the naïvely hopeful doctrines of the Enlightenment? Why do most people, and most historians, in backward and in advanced countries, in the capitalist world and in the Marxist world, still 'believe in progress'?

The appeal of the sheer technical virtuosity of modern societies, of the ever new marvels to lighten the burdens of existence, should not be underrated: at this shallow level, there is, of course, general agreement on progress, but much of the deeper certainties are also anchored here. Science (and the number of scientists) has grown exponentially, and with it has the number of works on progress. A bibliography of 1932, for example, listed sixteen titles on progress published before 1900, seventeen in the first decade of the new century, thirty-one in the second, and fifty-six in the third.[11]

Among the marvels of science we also expect solutions to problems which lie nearer to the moralist's field, for example in social organization and human psychology, though we do not expect complete or perfect solutions. A good example of the recurrent belief of the scientist that social problems have simple, 'scientific' solutions if only the unprejudiced scientist were allowed to deal with them, is H. G. Wells's *Work, Wealth and Happiness of Mankind*, published in 1932. The fact that problems in social organization seem to multiply faster than their solutions should not blind us to the astonishing progress of the social and administrative sciences. It is only seventy years ago that the Webbs found, when they decided to have political institutions taught at the newly-fledged London School of Economics, that all applicants were interested in political philosophy only and considered the proposal to concern themselves with contemporary problems an insult –

11. EARLE E. EUBANK, *The Concept of Sociology* (1932), pp. 513–18, quoted in Sidney B. Fay, 'The Idea of Progress', Pres. Address, *Amer. Historical Review*, 52 (1946–7), 231.

Yesterday interviewed candidates [Beatrice Webb noted in her diary for 14th July, 1896] ... all imagined that political science consisted of a knowledge of Aristotle and modern! writers such as De Tocqueville ... When Sidney [Webb] suggested a course of lectures to be prepared on different systems of municipal taxation, when Graham [Wallas] suggested a study of the rival methods of election from *ad hoc* to proportional representation, the wretched candidates looked aghast and thought evidently that we were amusing ourselves at their expense.[12]

Over a whole wide field, from welfare provisions to employment policies, and from urban planning to the setting up of the United Nations with its specialized agencies, there have been solutions found to problems of social organization which at the beginning of the century were not only not known, but not even conceived to be possible. It may well be true that the solutions limp behind the problems; but the idea of progress only demands improvement, not perfection, at any one stage.

Similarly, individual and social psychology have made enormous strides since, say, the beginning of the present century. If the advance is considered too slow, it is yet at least within a scientific and experimental framework rather than one depending on a preconceived philosophy of man. Also, significantly, progress has been most evident where the pressure to find answers has been greatest, e.g. in education, in intelligence testing and in 'industrial psychology' –

Men have found better ways, not only to dye a cloth or build a bridge, but to govern, teach and employ.[13]

Methods of human control and 'social engineering' have advanced as much in the past half-century as have the natural sciences, though their results are less spectacular, and still far less 'successful' in the sense of coming true to predictions. Yet within its limitations, the expectation of the Enlightenment has

12. *Our Partnership* (1948), p. 94.
13. B. F. SKINNER, 'The Design of Cultures', *Daedalus*, 90 (1961), 544.

been fulfilled: rational thought, the 'scientific method', has been applied to the social sciences and has proved capable of increasing man's power over his environment in this area also.

The historian, or the philosopher of history, however, who wishes to make sense of the past in order to determine his own conduct towards the future, is not thereby rescued from his dilemma. How safe are the 'predictions', the 'laws' of the social sciences? How far are they valid beyond the period in which they were made? Can any absolute values stand up to the changing judgements of history, and if they cannot, how can we live, how can we 'make' history without firm, eternal, or at least external, values?

Those of us who cannot blindly follow one or the other extreme offered to us are caught up in the inevitable duality of the historical experience, and of the historical understanding. The basis of that duality lies in the simultaneous truth of history as a series of events, and history as order: history as unique, and as repetitive; or, in Herder's terms, as synthetic and as part of a single chain of human development; and therefore, as determined by discoverable laws, and as subject to our choices and our wills. In the end, no philosophy which totally excludes one or the other of these opposites will stand up to investigation –

... if the stages of evolution were essentially diverse, the possibility of history is inconceivable; and if history were a manifestation of human phenomena where all but the accidental were simply the same, the interest it excites would in no respect be higher than the pleasure we take in an ordinary novel.[14]

This duality reappears in the nominal opposition between free will and determinism. An inchoate sequence of historical events could make no history, and could not be operated on by man. Man always assumes regularity in his environment, and all his actions are based on a purposive use of his rational environment.

14. F. H. BRADLEY, in 1874, quoted in Baillie, *The Belief in Progress* (1950), p. 167.

There never was a time when man took his practical environment to be unintelligible, and the picture of an indeterminate world has been the prerogative solely of philosophers.

But the area over which man has sought to obtain control has changed with his changing powers and his changing active role in a developing human society, and today it is extending into new dimensions. Today, as always, man is not 'free' to ignore the laws of nature, though he may remove some social constraint; and causation is not a command, but a description of what happens, including a description of man's own nature. Men have a will and a purpose, and act deliberately in society; how then can man as historian and social scientist claim to be able to predict this 'deliberate' action? The claim, we have seen earlier, was at one time attacked as an illegitimate attempt to infringe the liberty, the responsibility of man in history. Today, we are perhaps more inclined to attack it as leaving out the reflexive feedback, the self-consciousness of man as actor and simultaneously as observer. Will not the knowledge of social laws, the recognition of determinism, affect human action and destroy the expected regularity, to set up an unstable and unpredictable oscillation, a kind of poker game in which predictable elements are discounted and only the gamble of guessing each other's actions remains? Has not the very success of the social sciences destroyed the basis of their accuracy, as men become consciously organized, instead of being individualistic social atoms driven by predictable motives? In either case, the sheet-anchor of an independent value system is threatened: we must admit either that our free will is an illusion, or that our attempt at a scientific understanding of human history is doomed.

For those who can no longer hold to antiquated mythologies as the moral basis of their lives, it is here that the idea of progress has assumed its central position. The strength of this belief and its capacity to survive are to be explained precisely by the fact that it provides the moral anchor for which every soul craves, while at the same time resolving the intellectual doubts of historical interpretation, and fitting so many of the facts of observed technological, social and economic history. Gilbert Murray's sentiments are even more apt than when they were first pronounced –

. . . as to progress, it is no doubt a real fact. To many of us it is a truth that lies somewhere near the roots of our religion.[15]

It is because the anarchic results of innumerable wishes pulling in different directions can no longer be technically tolerated, and every society is forced to increase its social control, that a social purpose has become all the more imperative for the personal salvation of individuals. Simultaneously our scientific history convinces us that our purpose, and our freedom of action, can be served only by discovering the laws of historical development as best we may, and following them. The laws, as observed in recent centuries, point to progress in wealth, in knowledge, in control over nature. Recent historical experience supports the notion of a single world historical development, in which the advanced nations advance further, and the others follow their path to improvement. This result does not, at the least, conflict with the further observation that men each want their own good and wish to act in a way they consider 'right', and that as their power of achieving any of their aims is growing, their success in benefiting themselves is also likely to increase.

Yet this alone would not give the idea of progress its contemporary power. For in part, it is sustained by the spiritual needs of modern man who is searching for a meaning in this world –

In this predicament action, with its involvement and commitment, its being *engagé*, seemed to hold out the hope, not of solving any problems, but of making it possible to live with them.

Putting it therefore at its lowest, a modern philosophy is vastly

15. *Essays and Addresses* (1921), p. 19. But, Murray adds, progress 'never happens of its own accord'; it needs man's initiative, and there are, consequently, many relapses.

strengthened if it is based on a *task* for man, embracing humanity. And here we find that

only humans, if anyone, can ensure human progress beyond the caprices of an extrahuman will or the purposelessness of impersonal processes.

The only progress which we can care for is the progress which we ourselves bring about, or can believe that we bring about.

Even if it is true that 'Progress as an ideal of action cannot be precisely identical with Progress as a fact or object of actual or possible knowledge', and that 'observed progress is mainly technical, whereas believed progress is mainly spiritual',[16] it yet allows that a belief in progress is a spiritual necessity, because we need to believe in spiritual progress. Its very uncertainty supplies the spring for our action, for something completely predetermined ceases to have any moral meaning.

It is on this basis that all those who are heirs to the Western tradition can agree. The philosopher of the Enlightenment, who for the first time put hedonism and Utilitarianism into a social garb, and linked freedom and necessity by asserting that what was moral, was also rational, did so in the name of the progress of humanity. For the Marxist, progress is not simply a description, but a purpose to be fought for, for the most that can be assumed is the development of the socio-economic substructure; without purposive action, the superstructure might lag, lead or move in an opposite direction. His purpose is to create the realm of human freedom in which progress in a deeper sense will be possible. And even the modern liberal historian can see no other objective: 'The hope of an ultimate happy state on this planet to be enjoyed by future generations ... has replaced, as a social power, the hopes of felicity in another world,' wrote J. B. Bury,

16. HANNAH ARENDT, *Between Past and Future* (1954, English edn 1961), p. 9; J. A. MAZZEO, *Renaissance and Revolution* (1965, edn of 1967), p. 280; J. A. SMITH, 'Progress as an Ideal of Action', in F. S. Marvin (ed.), *Progress and History* (1916), pp. 299, 307; Baillie, p. 156.

and H. A. L. Fisher, who was more than any other historian associated with the view that history showed no pattern and no laws, followed that oft-quoted statement immediately with these words –

The fact of progress is written plain and large on the page of history; but progress is not a law of nature. The ground gained by one generation may be lost by the next [17]

Progress, like history itself, is not just an object of study: it is also a challenge. For those who are in the van of humanity, groping forward into the dark, the belief that they are moving in an upward direction is also a necessity. Today, the only possible alternative to the belief in progress would be total despair.

This generation finds itself once again at the meeting point of opposites. It has had the most powerful reasons for believing in human progress, as well as the most powerful reasons for despairing of it. We cannot reasonably assume that there will be no further relapse, but we can assume, with Pascal, that all humanity is as one life, always learning, always adding to its knowledge, and never quite forgetting the lessons of the past.

17. J. B. BURY, *The Idea of Progress* (1920), p. viii; H. A. L. FISHER, *History of Europe* (1946 edn), p. v.

BIBLIOGRAPHY

WHEREVER possible, English editions or translations have been selected, both for this bibliography and for the notes to the text. The selection has also been made with an eye to the accessibility of the works and editions included.

The Bibliography is divided for convenience into sections as follows. Many works straddle more than one section and will be found in the section considered most appropriate.

1. THE IDEA OF PROGRESS

Bloch, Ernst, *Differenzierungen im Begriff Fortschritt* (Berlin, 1956).

Bury, J. B., *The Idea of Progress* (1920).

Chambers, Clarke A., 'The Belief in Progress in Twentieth-Century America', *J. Hist. Ideas*, 19 (1958).

Bibliography

Delmage, Rutherford E., 'The American Idea of Progress, 1750–1800', *Proc. Amer. Philosophical Society*, 91 (1947).

Delvaille, J., *Essai sur Histoire de l'idée de progrès jusqu'à la fin du 18ième siècle* (Paris, 1910).

Doren, Charles van, *The Idea of Progress* (N.Y., 1967).

Fay, Sidney B., 'The Idea of Progress', *Amer. Historical Rev.*, 52 (1946–7).

Friedmann, Georges, *La Crise du progrès, 1895–1935* (Paris, 1936).

Ginsberg, Morris, *The Idea of Progress* (1953).

Hinton, R. W. K., 'Progress in the Twentieth Century', *Cambridge J.* I (1947–8).

Marvin, F. S., (ed.), *Progress and History* (1916).

Teggert, F. J., (ed.), *The Idea of Progress* (Readings), (Berkeley, 1949).

Varros, V. L., 'Human Progress, the Idea and the Reality' *Amer. J. of Sociology*, 21 (1915).

Welter, Rush, 'The Idea of Progress in America', *J. Hist. Ideas*, 16 (1955).

2. THEORIES OF HISTORY

Acton, Lord, *A Lecture on the Study of History* (1895).

Antoni, Carlo, *From History to Sociology* (Detroit, 1939).

Barnes, H. E., *A History of Historical Writings* (Norman, Okla., 1937).

Barraclough, G., *History and the Common Man* (1967).

Barraclough, G., *History in a Changing World* (Oxford, 1955).

Black, J. B., *The Art of History* (1962).

Butterfield, Herbert, *Man on his Past* (Cambridge, 1955).

Carr, E. H., *What is History?* (1961).

Cassirer, E., *The Problem of Knowledge* (New Haven, 1950).

Childe, V. Gordon, *What Happened in History* (1946).

Cohen, Morris R., 'Causation and its Applicaion to History', *J. Hist. Ideas*, 3 (1942).

Danto, A. C., *Analytical Philosophy of History* (Cambridge, 1965).

Dray, William H., *Philosophy of History* (Englewood Cliffs, N.J., 1964).

Finberg, H. P. R., (ed.), *Approaches to History* (1962).

Bibliography

Forbes, Duncan, 'Historismus in England', *Cambridge J.*, 4 (1951).

Frankel, Charles, *The Case for Modern Man* (1957).

Fussner, F. Smith, *The Historical Revolution* (1962).

Gardiner, Patrick, (ed.), *Theories of History* (Readings), (Glencoe, Ill., 1959).

Hale, J. R., *The Evolution of British Historiography* (1967).

Hempel, Carl G., 'The Function of General Laws in History', *J. Philosophy* (1942).

Hodson, Marshall G. S., 'The Interrelations of Societies in History', *Comparative Studies in Society and History*, 5 (1962–3).

Hook, S., *The Hero in History* (1945).

Huizinga, J., *Im Bann der Geschichte* (Basel, 1943).

Klibansky, R. and Paton, H. J. (Eds.), *Philosophy and History* (Oxford, 1936).

Mandelbaum, M., *The Problem of Historical Knowledge* (N.Y., 1938).

Marcus, John T., 'Time and the Sense of History: East and West', *Comparative Studies in Society and History*, 3 (1960–61).

Meinecke, F., *Die Entstehung des Historismus* (2 vols., Munich, Oldenburg, 1946, 1959).

Schevill, Ferdinand, *Six Historians* (Chicago, 1956).

White, Morton, *Foundations of Historical Knowledge* (N.Y., 1965).

Wittram, R., *Das Interesse an der Geschichte* (Göttingen, 1958).

3. THE CLASSICAL, MEDIEVAL AND EARLY MODERN PERIODS

Augustine, St, *The City of God* (2 vols., 1962 edn).

Bacon, Francis, *Works* (7 vols., 1879–90).

Durand, Dana B., 'Tradition and Innovation in Fifteenth-Century Italy', *J. Hist. Ideas*, 4 (1943).

Ghosh, Oroon K., 'Some Theories of Universal History', *Comparative Studies in Society and History*, 7 (1964–5).

Grant, Edward, 'Late Medieval Thought, Copernicus and the Scientific Revolution', *J. Hist. Ideas*, 23 (1962).

Hall, A. R., *Scientific Revolution, 1500–1800* (1954).

Keller, A. C., 'Zilsel, the Artisans, and the Idea of Progress in the Renaissance', *J. Hist. Ideas*, 11 (1950).

Mazzeo, J. A., *Renaissance and Revolution* (1967).

McRae, Robert, 'The Unity of the Sciences: Bacon, Descartes and Leibniz', *J. Hist. Ideas*, 18 (1967).

Mommsen, Theodor E., 'St Augustine and the Christian Idea of Progress', *J. Hist. Ideas*, 12 (1951).

Sypher, G. Wylie, 'Similarities between the Scientific and the Historical Revolutions at the End of the Renaissance', *J. Hist. Ideas*, 26 (1965).

Toulmin, Stephen and Goodfield, June, *The Discovery of Time* (paperback, 1967).

Tuveson, E. L., *Millennium and Utopia. A Study in the Background of the Idea of Progress* (Berkeley and Los Angeles, 1949).

4. THE FRENCH ENLIGHTENMENT

Becker, C. L., *The Heavenly City of the Eighteenth Century Philosophers* (New Haven, 1932).

Bossuet, J. B., *An Universal History* (1778).

Brumfitt, J. H., *Voltaire: Historian* (Oxford, 1958).

Cassirer, Ernst, *The Philosophy of the Enlightenment* (Princeton, N.J., 1951, 1st edn 1932).

Chastellux, Marquis de, *Essays on Public Happiness* (2 vols., 1790).

Condorcet, A. N. de, *Sketch for a Historical Picture of the Progress of the Human Mind* (1955).

Condorcet, A. N. de, *Vie de Monsieur Turgot* (Paris, 1786).

Edsall, H. L., *The Idea of Progress and History in Fontenelle and Voltaire* (New Haven, 1941).

Frankel, Charles, *The Faith of Reason* (N.Y., 1948).

Frazer, J. G., *Condorcet on the Progress of the Human Mind* (Oxford, 1933).

Henry, Charles, *Correspondance ... Condorcet et Turgot, 1770–1779* (Paris, 1883).

Hubert, René, *Les Sciences Sociales dans l'Encyclopédie* (Lille, 1923).

Koyré, Alexander, 'Condorcet', *J. Hist. Ideas*, 9 (1948).

Ladd, Everett C., Jr, 'Helvétius and D'Holbach, la moralisation de la politique', *J. Hist. Ideas*, 23 (1962).

Marsak, Leonard M., 'Bernard de Fontenelle: in Defense of Science', *J. Hist. Ideas*, 20 (1959).

Martin, Kingsley, *French Liberal Thought in the Eighteenth Century* (1929).

Morley, John, *Critical Miscellanies* (vol. 2, 1886).

Montesquieu, C. de, *The Spirit of the Laws* (2 vols., 1878).

Rosenthal, Jerome, 'Voltaire's Philosophy of History', *J. Hist. Ideas*, 16 (1955).

Rousseau, J. J., *A Discourse on the Origin of Inequality*, in *The Social Contract and Discourses* (1932).

Saint-Pierre, Charles I. C., *Projet de Paix Perpétuelle* (Utrecht, 1713).

Sampson, R. V., *Progress in the Age of Reason* (Cambridge, Mass., 1957).

Stromberg, R. N., 'History in the Eighteenth Century', *J. Hist. Ideas*, 12 (1951).

Stephens, W. W., *Life and Writings of Turgot* (1895).

Turgot, A. R. J., 'Plan de deux discours sur l'histoire universelle', in *Oeuvres* (ed. Schelle, vol. 1, Paris, 1913).

Turgot, A. R. J., *The Progress of the Human Mind* (Hanover, New Hampshire, 1929).

Vico, G., *The New Science of Giambattista Vico* (Ithaca, N.Y., 1948).

Voltaire, *La Philosophie de la histoire* (Geneva, 1963).

5. THE SCOTTISH AND ENGLISH ENLIGHTENMENT AND THE ECONOMISTS

Bolingbroke, Henry St J., *Letters on the Study and Use of History* (1779).

Brailsford, H. N., *Shelley, Godwin and their Circle* (1915).

Brown, Ira V., *Joseph Priestley, Selections from his Writings* (Pennsylvania, 1962).

Bryson, Gladys, *Man and Society: The Scottish Enquiry of the Eighteenth Century* (Princeton, N.J., 1945).

Burke, Edmund, *Works* (8 vols., 1852).

Canavan, Francis P., *The Political Reason of Edmund Burke* (Durham, N.C., 1960).

Clark, J. M., *et al.*, *Adam Smith, 1776–1926* (Chicago, 1928).

Cobban, A., *Edmund Burke and the Revolt against the Eighteenth Century* (1929).

Ferguson, Adam, *Essay on the History of Civil Society* (1777 edn).

Bibliography

Ferguson, Adam, *Principles of Moral and Political Science* (Edinburgh, 1792).

Godwin, W., *Enquiry Concerning Political Justice* (Toronto, 1946).

Hume, David, *Essays, Moral, Political and Literary* (1903 edn).

Hume, David, *Writings on Economics* (1955).

Lehmann, W. C., *John Millar of Glasgow* (Cambridge, 1960).

Owen, Robert, *A New View of Society and Other Essays* (1927 edn).

Peardon, T. P., *The Transition in English Historical Writing 1760–1830* (N.Y., 1933).

Polanyi, Karl, *The Great Transformation* (Boston, Mass., 1944).

Priestley, F. E. L., *Notes on Godwin's Political Justice* (Toronto, 1946).

Priestley, Joseph, *Lectures on History and General Policy* (Birmingham, 1783).

Robertson, J. G., *Studies in the Genesis of Romantic Theory in the Eighteenth Century* (Cambridge, 1923).

Skinner, A., 'Economics and History', *Scottish J. of Political Economy*, 12 (1965).

Smith, Adam, *An Inquiry into the Nature and Causes of the Wealth of Nations* (2 vols., 1904 edn).

Smith, Adam, *Theory of Moral Sentiments* (2 vols., 1804 edn).

Stephen, Leslie, *English Thought in the Eighteenth Century* (2 vols., 1876).

6. GERMAN IDEALISM

Clark, R. T. Jr, *Herder: His Life and Thought* (Berkeley and L. A., 1955).

Hegel, G. W. F., *Lectures on the Philosophy of History* (N.Y., 1944).

Herder, J. G., *Outline of a Philosophy of the History of Man* (1803 edn).

Kant, E., 'The Idea of a Universal History', translated De Quincey, in *Works* (1897), vol. 9.

Lessing, G. E., *The Education of the Human Race* (1896).

Spitz, Lewis W., 'Natural Law and the Theory of History in Herder', *J. Hist. Ideas*, 16 (1953).

7. SAINT-SIMON TO JOHN STUART MILL

Comte, Auguste, *A Discourse on the Positive Spirit* (1903).

Comte, Auguste, *A System of Positive Polity* (1875-7).

Durkheim, E., *Socialism and Saint-Simon* (1959).

Iggers, George G., *The Cult of Authority. The Political Philosophy of the Saint-Simonians* (Hague, 1958).

Letwin, Shirley Robin, *The Pursuit of Certainty* (Cambridge, 1965).

Manuel, F. E., *The New World of Henri Saint-Simon* (Cambridge, Mass., 1956).

Manuel, F. E., *The Prophets of Paris* (Cambridge, Mass., 1962).

Martineau, H., *The Positive Philosophy of Auguste Comte* (2 vols., 1875).

Marvin, F. S., *Comte, the Founder of Sociology* (N.Y., 1937).

Mill, J. S., *Auguste Comte and Positivism* (1865).

Mill, J. S., *Dissertations and Discussions* (4 vols., 1859-75).

Mill, J. S., *The Spirit of the Age* (Chicago, 1942).

Mill, J. S., *A System of Logic* (1843).

Mueller, I. W., *John Stuart Mill and French Thought* (Urbana, Ill., 1956).

Pankhurst, R. K. P., *The Saint-Simonians, Mill and Carlyle* (1957).

Plamenatz, J., *The English Utilitarians* (Oxford, 1949).

Proudhon, P. J., *Philosophie du Progrès* (Paris, 1946).

Saint-Simon, C. H. de, *The Doctrine of Saint-Simon, an Exposition* (Boston, Mass., 1958).

Saint-Simon, C. H. de, *Oeuvres* (6 vols., Paris, 1966).

Simon, Walter M., 'History for Utopia: Saint-Simon and the Idea of Progress', *J. Hist. Ideas*, 17 (1956).

8. MARX AND THE LATER SOCIALISTS

Bottomore, T. B., and Rubel, M., (eds.), *Select Writings in Sociology and Social Philosophy* (1956).

Cole, G. D. H., *A History of Socialist Thought* (7 vols., 1953-60).

Daniels, R. V., 'Fate and Will in the Marxian Philosophy of History', *J. Hist. Ideas*, 21 (1960).

Engels, F., *Anti-Dühring* (1943).

Engels, F., *Ludwig Feuerbach and the Outcome of Classical German Philosophy* (Moscow, 1946).

Bibliography

Hook, S., *From Hegel to Marx* (N.Y., 1935).

Krieger, Leonard, 'Marx and Engels as Historians', *J. Hist. Ideas*, 14 (1953).

Marx, K., *Capital* (2 vols., 1939 edn).

Marx, K., *Critique of the Gotha Programme* (1941).

Marx, K., *Critique of Political Economy* (Chicago, 1913).

Marx, K., *The Poverty of Philosophy* (1941).

Marx and Engels, *Correspondence* (1941).

Marx and Engels, *The German Ideology* (1942).

Plamenatz, J., *Man and Society* (2 vols., vol. 2, 1963).

Plekhanov, G. V., *The Materialist Conception of History* (1940).

Wilson, Edmund, *To the Finland Station* (paperback, 1960).

9. DARWIN, SPENCER AND VICTORIAN OPTIMISM

Bagehot, Walter, *Physics and Politics* (1903).

Bonar, James, *Philosophy and Political Economy* (1893).

Buckle, H. T., *History of Civilization in England* (1904).

Checkland, S. G., 'Growth and Progress: The Nineteenth-Century View in Britain', *Econ. Hist. Rev.*, 2nd S., 12 (1959).

Childe, V. Gordon, *Social Evolution* (1951).

Darwin, Charles, *The Origin of Species* (1950).

Draper, John W., *A History of the Intellectual Development of Europe* (2 vols., 1875).

Hobhouse, L. T., *Social Development* (1924).

Huxley, Julian, *Evolution, the Modern Synthesis* (1942).

Maine, H. J. S., *Ancient Law* (1912).

Morgan, L. H., *Ancient Society* (Cleveland, 1963).

Roberston, J. M., *Buckle and his Critics* (1895).

Rumney, Jay, *Herbert Spencer's Sociology* (N.Y., 1966).

St Aubyn, G., *A Victorian Eminence. The Life and Work of Henry Thomas Buckle* (1958).

Spencer, Herbert, 'Progress, its Law and Cause', in *Essays, Scientific, Political and Speculative* (3 vols., 1868–78).

Spencer, Herbert, *Social Statics* (1868).

Wells, G. A., 'Critics of Buckle', *Past and Present*, 9 (1956).

Bibliography

10. THE OPPONENTS OF HISTORICAL SCIENCE

Bendix, Reinhard, *Max Weber, an Intellectual Portrait* (1966).

Berlin, I., *Historical Inevitability* (Oxford, 1964).

Burckhardt, J., *Force and Freedom* (N.Y., 1955).

Collingwood, R. G., *The Idea of History* (Oxford, 1946).

Croce, B., *My Philosophy and Other Essays* (1949).

Dilthey, W., *The Essence of Philosophy* (Chapel Hill, N.C., 1954).

Gasset, Ortega y., *History as a System and Other Essays* (N.Y., 1961).

Gasset, Ortega y., *Toward a Philosophy of History* (N.Y., 1941).

Hayek, F. A. v., *The Counterrevolution of Science* (Glencoe, Ill., 1952).

Maritain, Jacques, *On the Philosophy of History* (N.Y., 1957).

Mises, L. v., *Theory and History* (New Haven, Conn., 1957).

Niebuhr, R., *Faith and History* (N.Y., 1949).

Popper, K. R., *The Open Society and Its Enemies* (2 vols., 1945).

Popper, K. R., *The Poverty of Historicism* (1957).

11. THE PESSIMISTS

Africa, Thomas W., 'The City of God Revisited: Toynbee's Considerations', *J. Hist. Ideas*, 23 (1962).

Collingwood, R. G., 'Oswald Spengler and the Theory of Historical Cycles', *Antiquity*, 1 (1927).

Danilewski, N. I., *Russland und Europa* (Stuttgart, 1920).

Falnes, Oscar J., 'European Progress and the "Superior Races": As Viewed by a fin-de-siècle Liberal, Charles H. Pearson', *J. Hist. Ideas*, 15 (1954).

Hughes, H. Stuart, *Oswald Spengler* (N.Y., 1952).

Levin, Samuel M., 'Malthus and the Idea of Progress', *J. Hist. Ideas*, 27 (1966).

MacMaster, Robert E., *Danilevsky. A Russian Totalitarian Philosopher* (Cambridge, Mass., 1967).

Malthus, T. R., *Essay on Population* (1826).

Montagu, M. F. Ashley (ed.), *Toynbee and History* (Readings) (Boston, Mass., 1956).

Sorel, Georges, *Les Illusions de progrès* (Paris, 1908).

Sorokin, P. A., *Social Philosophies of an Age of Crisis* (1950, English edn 1952).

Spengler, O., *The Decline of the West* (2 vols., N.Y., 1926–8).

Spengler, O., *Man and Technics* (N.Y., 1932).

Toynbee, A. J., *America and the World Revolution* (1962).

Toynbee, A. J., *Civilization on Trial* (Oxford, 1948).

Toynbee, A. J., *The Economy of the Western Hemisphere* (1962).

Toynbee, A. J., *The Present-day Experiment in Western Civilization* (1962).

Toynbee, A. J., *A Study of History* (10 vols., plus 2 additional vols., Oxford, 1934–1961).

Toynbee, A. J., *A Study of History, Abridgement*, by D. C. Somervell (2 vols., Oxford, 1946, 1957).

Trevor-Roper, H. R., 'Arnold Toynbee's Millennium', *Encounter*, 8 (1957).

12. ECONOMIC DEVELOPMENT

Cairncross, A. K., *Factors in Economic Development* (paperback 1964).

Clark, Colin, *The Conditions of Economic Progress* (1951).

Clough, Shephard B., *The Rise and Fall of Civilization* (1953).

Dupriez, Léon H., and Hague, D. C. (eds.), *Economic Progress* (Louvain, 1955).

Galbraith, J. K., *Economic Development* (Cambridge, Mass., 1964).

Galbraith, J. K., *The New Industrial State* (1967).

Gerschenkron, A., *Economic Backwardness in Historical Perspective* (Cambridge, Mass., 1962).

Kuznets, S., *Economic Growth and Structure* (1965).

Meier, C. M., and Baldwin, R. E., *Economic Development: Theory, History, Policy* (N.Y., 1962).

Rostow, W. W., *The Stages of Economic Growth* (Cambridge, 1961).

Shmelev, N. P., 'A Critique of Bourgeois Theories of Economic Development', *J. Development Studies*, 1 (1964).

Sievers, Allen M., *Revolution, Evolution and the Economic Order* (New Jersey, 1962).

Spiegel, H., 'Theories of Economic Development: History and Classification', *J. Hist. Ideas*, 16 (1953).

13. RECENT THOUGHT ON THE IDEA OF PROGRESS

Arendt, Hannah, *Between Past and Future* (1961).

Baillie, John, *The Belief in Progress* (1950).

Becker, Carl, *Progress and Power* (N.Y., 1965).

Brown, Harrison, *The Challenge of Man's Future* (N.Y., 1956).

Daedalus, 90/3 (1961), Issue devoted to 'Evolution and Man's Progress'.

Dawson, C. H., *The Dynamics of World History* (1957).

Inge, W. R., *The Idea of Progress* (Oxford, 1920).

Mannheim, K., *Ideology and Utopia* (N.Y., 1936).

Mounier, Emmanuel, *Be not afraid* (1951).

Salomon, Albert, *The Tyranny of Progress* (N.Y., 1955).

Selsam, Howard, *Ethics and Progress* (N.Y., 1965).

Whyte, L. L., *The Next Development in Man* (N.Y., 1950).

INDEX

Index

Economic development *see* Development theories

Economic growth, 188–91

Economic History, 33–5, 54, 103, 144, 173

Economics *see* Political economy

Education and progress, 45, 51, 58, 83, 87, 92, 147, 191

Empiricism, 66

Encyclopédie, encyclopedists, 32, 39, 42–3, 44, 47, 48, 49, 51–2, 53, 58, 77

Enfantin, B. P., 114

Engels, F., 126–35, 155, 195

Enlightenment, 13, 24, 25, 31, 103, 111, 116, 127, 137, 144–5, 151, 166, 168, 170, 181, 183, 184, 186, 198–9, 200, 204

Entrepreneurship, 66, 76, 105

Epicureans, 16

Evolution, 104, 120, 140–41, 146, 197–8

Ferguson, A., 33, 39, 66–7, 158, 161, 171

Feudalism, feudal society, 27, 50, 74, 76, 112, 115, 118, 120, 132, 134, 136

Fichte, J. G., 97, 98

Fontenelle, B., le B., 40

Free will in history, 97–8, 147, 154, 155–9, 201–2

French Revolution, 100, 103, 104, 105, 112

Gasset, Ortega y, 152

Gibbon, E., 33, 59–60, 74

Godwin, W., 53, 66, 80–82, 166, 186, 195

'Golden Age', 16, 19, 42, 112

Great men in history, 123, 153–4

Greek view of history, 16–17, 78

Happiness, 96 (*see also* Utilitarianism)

Hayek, F. A. v., 153, 161, 162, 163

Hegel, G. W. F., 97–99, 114, 127

Helvétius, C. A., 45–7

Herder, J. G., 95–6, 180, 201

Hildebrand, B., 137

Historical school of economists, 136–8, 139

Historicism, 38–9, 93, 114, 138, 152–3

Historiography, metaphysical, 98; scientific *see* Scientific history

Hobhouse, L. T., 121

Humboldt, K. W. v., 100

Hume, D., 34, 60–66, 70, 96, 122, 155, 166

Hutcheson, F., 71

Idealist philosophy of history, 39, 58, 93, 96–8, 99–100, 104, 127

Inge, Dean W. R., 197

Judaic view of progress, 17, 178

Kames, Lord H. H., 69

Kant, I., 94–5, 96, 98, 147, 154

Knies, K., 137

Lamarckian theory, 49, 95, 143

Laws of history, 97, 102, 109, 123–4, 130, 142, 144, 145–7; based on Newtonian physics, 20, 24, 36–7, 118; distinguishing the general and the unique, 56, 86; necessary for present-day belief in progress, 151, 154, 157–8, 160, 202, 204–5

Laws in social sciences, 36, 44, 56, 59, 60–61, 66–8, 85–7, 102, 104, 123–4, 136–8, 140, 146–7, 153–5, 157–61, 163, 201–2; *see also* Regularities of large numbers

Leibniz, G. W., 24, 119

Lessing, G. E., 97, 98

List, F., 136

MORE ABOUT PENGUINS
AND PELICANS

Penguinews, which appears every month, contains details of all the new books issued by Penguins as they are published. From time to time it is supplemented by *Penguins in Print*, which is a complete list of all available books published by Penguins. (There are well over three thousand of these.)

A specimen copy of *Penguinews* will be sent to you free on request, and you can become a subscriber for the price of the postage. For a year's issues (including the complete lists) please send 30p if you live in the United Kingdom, or 60p if you live elsewhere. Just write to Dept EP, Penguin Books Ltd, Harmondsworth, Middlesex, enclosing a cheque or postal order, and your name will be added to the mailing list.

Note: *Penguinews* and *Penguins in Print* are not available in the U.S.A. or Canada

Another Pelican by Sidney Pollard

THE GENESIS OF MODERN MANAGEMENT

In the cut-throat competition of the Industrial Revolution many capitalists saw the need for 'managers' – employees paid to plan profits, keep accounts and mould men to the new machines. Living down their rascally reputation for dishonesty, these supervisors eventually came to constitute a new class, as essential and practical a part of the impetus to industrialism as the working class itself. This volume in the Pelican Library of Business and Management is a unique study of this early managerial revolution, of the problems which confronted the first generation of managers and of the complex interactions of mass-production technology and human organization. An important contribution to developmental economics, it is also a convincing analysis of the historical factors which continue to condition the present-day practices of British management.

In the Pelican Library of Business and Management